CVs
pat scudamore
and
hilton catt

For over 60 years, more than 40 million people have learnt over 750 subjects the **teach yourself** way, with impressive results.

be where you want to be with **teach yourself**

For UK order enquiries: please contact Bookpoint Ltd, 130 Milton Park, Abingdon, Oxon OX14 4SB. Telephone: +44 (0) 1235 827720. Fax: +44 (0) 1235 400454. Lines are open 09.00–18.00, Monday to Saturday, with a 24-hour message answering service. Details about our titles and how to order are available at www.teachyourself.co.uk

For USA order enquiries: please contact McGraw-Hill Customer Services, PO Box 545, Blacklick, OH 43004-0545, USA. Telephone: 1-800-722-4726. Fax: 1-614-755-5645.

For Canada order enquiries: please contact McGraw-Hill Ryerson Ltd, 300 Water St, Whitby, Ontario L1N 9B6, Canada. Telephone: 905 430 5000. Fax: 905 430 5020.

Long renowned as the authoritative source for self-guided learning – with more than 40 million copies sold worldwide – the **teach yourself** series includes over 300 titles in the fields of languages, crafts, hobbies, business, computing and education.

British Library Cataloguing in Publication Data: a catalogue record for this title is available from the British Library.

Library of Congress Catalog Card Number: on file.

First published in UK 2004 by Hodder Arnold, 338 Euston Road, London, NW1 3BH.

First published in US 2004 by Contemporary Books, a Division of the McGraw-Hill Companies, 1 Prudential Plaza, 130 East Randolph Street, Chicago, IL 60601 USA.

This edition published 2004.

The **teach yourself** name is a registered trade mark of Hodder Headline Ltd.

Copyright © 2004 Pat Scudamore and Hilton Catt

Typeset by Transet Limited, Coventry, England.
Printed in Great Britain for Hodder Arnold, a division of Hodder Headline, 338 Euston Road, London NW1 3BH, by Cox & Wyman Ltd, Reading, Berkshire.

Hodder Headline's policy is to use papers that are natural, renewable and recyclable products and made from wood grown in sustainable forests. The logging and manufacturing processes are expected to conform to the environmental regulations of the country of origin.

Impression number   10 9 8 7 6 5 4 3 2 1
Year   2010 2009 2008 2007 2006 2005 2004

contents

introduction

Though it seems scarcely believable today, a job applicant with a CV (curiculum vitae) was a comparative rarity 25 years ago. Those with CVs tended to be:

- someone operating at the very top end of the job market, for example, a candidate for a senior management position
- someone with the funds or connections to have a CV professionally prepared
- alternatively someone with the backing of a firm of consultants – people who would put together a CV as part of their strategy for marketing a candidate to their clients.

How times have changed! Now we live in an age where practically everyone has a CV, irrespective of who they are, how much money they have or what occupational group they belong to. Why have CVs taken off with such momentum? There are five main reasons:

1 The stiff competition in the job market, to the extent where getting on the interview list in competitive employment situations is one of the biggest hurdles candidates have to face. This has generated the need to put more effort into the way we present ourselves to employers, and resulted in the correctly held view that a good CV is what can make the difference when it comes to opening doors.

2 'Send a copy of your CV...' is the standard tailpiece to almost every job advertisement – you're stumped from the start if you don't have one.

3 The growth of home PC ownership and the availability of relatively low cost, high quality inkjet or laser printers has brought professional looking CVs within reach of almost anyone who is prepared to give it a go.

4 There is an abundance of help and advice available on the subject of preparing CVs – including books, ready-made CVs that you can download off the internet, and advice given to job seekers from sources such as outplacement counsellors, public employment services, etc.

5 The use of CVs for purposes other than job hunting is spreading. For instance a freelancer, self-employed contractor or someone seeking to source work for a small knowledge-based business might be asked to submit a CV as evidence of their skills and competence.

What this means is that, unless you are an absolute newcomer to the world of work, you will probably already have a CV. So, the two questions foremost in your mind as you pick up this book will be, 'Am I going to learning anything new?' and 'How will this knowledge benefit me?'

Teach Yourself CVs is a new look at producing CVs, and it will work for you across a wide range of situations. Whether your aim is to use your CV to attack markets where the competition is going to be intense, or you are seeking to make giant leaps in your career by getting headhunted, the answers are here for you.

An effective CV is one that addresses and accomplishes the task that you want it to perform. Defining this task is the all-important subject of Chapter 1. From this starting point, we will take you through what you need to put in your CV and, in some cases, what to leave out! Once you've got your CV down on paper, we will turn your attention to how you can put it to use – how to get it to work for you consistent with the aims you've set yourself. Our final chapter is about good CV management: keeping your CV up to date.

One of the less welcome developments of recent years has been the tendency for everyone's CV to look the same, to the point where any trace of individuality is obliterated. A central message in this book is that individuality is good. That 'little bit of you':

• makes your CV interesting
• gives employers and other recipients of your CV something they can latch on to and engage with.

The power of you is therefore an important force and one we shall be looking to harness within the design of your CV.

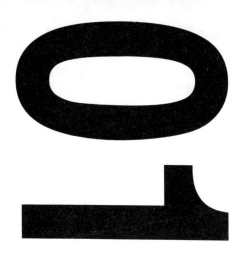

01

the task you face

In this chapter you will learn:
- what your CV is there to do for you
- how to use your CV to make a good first impression
- the importance of 'engagement factors' and how to get these to work for you

What you want your CV to do for you

What is a CV for? If you put this question to a cross-section of job seekers it's a safe bet most of them will answer, 'To get you interviews'. But is this necessarily the case? Let's take a look at six examples – six people who for different reasons are all faced with the task of having to sit down and put together a CV.

Example A: Anji
Anji is a sales high-flyer working in the telecommunications industry. She is 28 and keen to maximize her earnings potential by applying for any highly paid sales jobs that she sees advertised in national newspapers and on websites of leading telecommunications companies.

Example B: Doug
Doug is employed as a design engineer by a company who make special purpose machinery for the automotive industry. Doug feels he has no prospects and, for this reason, he is looking to make a move. Doug has decided to send his CV to the ten leading machine manufacturers in his area to see what opportunities they may have for him.

Example C: Lee
Lee is a 32-year-old management accountant who works for a company in the pharmaceuticals industry. There have been rumours flying around for some time that the company is set to merge with one of its biggest rivals. Lee is concerned that his job may no longer be safe, to the point where he feels the time has now come to put some irons in the fire. Lee plans to register with three firms of recruitment consultants who specialize in accountancy appointments, and he needs a CV for this purpose.

Example D: Gareth
Gareth is the general manager of a food wholesaling business – a position he has held for the last eight years. Though Gareth is perfectly happy in the job he is doing, he has just received an approach from a headhunter who is seeking to find out if he would be interested in a top management position with one of the major players in the industry and, if so, they would like him to submit a CV. Gareth is intrigued. Though he doesn't know yet whether he would take the job or not, he certainly wants to find out more.

Example E: Wendy

Wendy is a materials technologist who has been employed in the foundry industry since she graduated from university ten years ago. Her company is the last working foundry in her part of the world and there has just been an announcement that it is going to close at the end of the year. Wendy's partner Richard has a good job locally, so relocation to another part of the country is not an option she wishes to consider. Instead, Wendy has decided upon a complete change of career and she needs a CV to help her move into a fresh field.

Example F: Karen

Karen is a self-employed IT trainer who is seeking to source more work. She has recently made an approach to the operations manager of a large company that has leased premises on a new science park in the town where she lives. As a consequence of this approach, she has been asked to submit a copy of her CV so that her credentials as a training provider can be considered.

Define the task

What is immediately striking about Anji, Doug, Lee, Gareth, Wendy and Karen is that the task each one faces is very different.

- **Anji** is planning to attack a visible market (well-paid jobs that have been given prominent advertising). The task she faces therefore is one of *engaging* and *overcoming* competition. Getting on the interview list won't be easy, and the design of her CV needs to take this into account.

- **Doug** is about to set out on a fishing trip. By writing to a few selected employers, he is hoping to find out what's out there for him – if anything. His problem won't be competition: the main challenge he faces is getting across to the people he writes to (a) where he's coming from; and (b) what he's seeking to achieve. Without this information, recipients of Doug's unsolicited CV will have no way of knowing whether his ambitions match up with anything they can offer. In Doug's case, interviews are only any good if they have the prospect of leading somewhere.

- **Lee** needs a CV to enlist the help of three firms of consultants who can address the task of finding him another job if his fears of redundancy turn out to be well-founded. His CV needs to make clear to the consultants: (a) his situation; (b) his most marketable talents; and (c) what kind of positions would interest him.

- **Gareth**'s position is altogether different. He wasn't actively looking for another job when he got the call from the headhunter, but he's correctly identified that he needs to keep the process rolling. Being headhunted for a top job presents all of us with a golden opportunity to bargain for a good deal. Employers who go to the expense and trouble of hiring professional headhunters do so in the knowledge that at some stage they will have to negotiate job terms with the individual they target (terms that are going to be acceptable). Therefore, getting an interview is not the main issue with Gareth. The top priority of any CV he's asked to put together is to make his bargaining position known (the starting point for any negotiation).

- **Wendy** wants to make a career change. Her CV needs to have the capacity to open doors in sectors of the job market where she has no experience.

- **Karen** is the odd one out. Her need for a CV has nothing to do with job hunting. She is seeking to get work for herself from new clients (people who don't know her) and her CV is going to be used to vet her suitability.

Key point

Make your CV fit the task

Our six examples illustrate that CVs are used for a wide variety of purposes and across a wide range of situations. Consequently, to start off by following the 'one size fits all' approach to designing a CV is a mistake. Instead, *before* you put pen to paper you need to turn your thoughts to what you want your CV to do for you. If, like Anji, you want it to see off the competition, this is a defined aim and one that you can address. Similarly if, like Gareth, you want to make the most of being headhunted, this is another defined aim requiring a different approach.

Notepad

If you look at the chapter headings in this book, you will see that we deal with CVs according to the purpose for which they are intended. This is in line with our six examples and the chapters are as follows:

The importance of first impressions

What else do you need to consider before you sit down to the job of putting a CV together?

In some situations, the recipient of your CV will be someone who knows you or, alternatively, someone who knows you through a third party such as a consultant or a business associate. If your reputation is already made, there's no problem. In most cases, however, your CV will give the first impression of you to someone who could go on to play an important part in your future.

What's so special about first impressions? Two things:

1 Good or bad, they are the impressions that tend to stick.
2 Once formed, they're very hard to shift.

This means that your CV plays a vital part in anything that might follow. With a job application, for example, a good first impression formed from your CV will pave the way forward, for instance, to an interview. Conversely, a bad first impression will be almost impossible to recover from (consignment to the shredding machine is the most likely outcome!).

Halo effects

Professional interviewers are taught to be wary of halo effects, and this is why you need to know about them. Halo effects describe the tendency to see some good points in a candidate in the early stages of a selection process and from there on to ignore any flaws that arise. Halo effects also work in reverse. Where bad points are in evidence early on, any good points that arise later get skipped over.

Halo effects underline the message about good first impressions. In short, one of the jobs of your CV is to get the halo effects working in your favour and not against you.

Use your CV to project a good first impression

Going back to the task you face when designing a CV, one of the most important issues you need to address is the impression your CV is going to make when it lands on someone's desk. Will it do you justice? Or will it let you down and undermine your effort?

Here is a list of do's and don't's on presentation when it comes to preparing a CV – this will help you to avoid some of the more common mistakes people make and to ensure that your CV makes a good first impression when it arrives at its destination.

- DO use black ink on standard white A4 paper. This is not just a point of style. Your CV may need to be faxed or photocopied, and coloured print or paper doesn't do either satisfactorily. Flimsy paper or paper which is too thick (some people print their CVs on card) can be difficult to put through a fax machine. The same applies to odd-sized paper.
- DON'T handwrite CVs. It looks old-fashioned and furthermore you lose the capacity to edit and make corrections.
- DON'T succumb to the temptation to use fancy fonts and graphics. Keep it plain. Keep it simple.
- DON'T try to save space by resorting to font sizes that will have your readers searching for their glasses (or conversely not bothering).
- DO take care when printing off, especially on inkjet printers where blots and smudges can be a problem.
- DO print off a fresh copy of your CV every time you need one (photocopies don't have the same crispness).
- DON'T recycle CVs. If one is returned to you, bin it immediately.
- DO make sure that every CV you send out is in mint, pristine condition.
- DO be careful where you store CVs. A waft of stale cigarette smoke or fried food as the envelope is opened at the other end won't do much for you on the first impressions front!
- DO watch your grammar and spelling. Spell checkers are great but they may not tell you, for example, if you've given a proper word the wrong meaning. If your English does leave a little to be desired, ask someone with a good command of grammar and spelling to read through a draft. Needless to say, bad spelling and the wrong use of words won't do you any favours on a first impression.

- DO remember to keep your CV relevant and concise. There will be much more on this subject as you work your way through this book, but for now be aware that a long CV which rambles all over the place will not make the right impact.
- DO put your CV in an envelope the same size when mailing to avoid folding.

Engagement factors

What are engagement factors? In a nutshell these are the factors in selection that cause employers to take a shine to some candidates and not to others. Employers see something they like and they latch on to it. The chemistry clicks and, without question, this process of engagement has a considerable bearing on how far an individual candidate's application is going to progress as it moves through the various stages of selection.

Make your CV interesting

In the introduction, we drew your attention to the tendency in recent years for everyone's CV to look the same and, in part, this reflects the growing use of standard formats which people can access from sources such as books or websites. Unfortunately, however, the effect on the reader of all this sameness can be quite mind-numbing – particularly if they happen to have a big pile of CVs to read. The same phrases and buzz words crop up over and over again. The names, the employment histories and the aspirations all start to blur into one.

Key point
Think about your reader

When you prepare a CV, focus on making it interesting. Particularly in competitive employment situations, you need some way to make your CV stand out from the rest, and you won't do this by boring whoever is going to read it. So, next time you feel tempted to use a CV you've lifted from one of the popular texts or downloaded from the internet, think twice.

The need to keep it short

One message that has got through to people who prepare their own CVs is the need to keep it concise. As with all good advice, this can be taken too far, and we are now seeing one-page CVs where conciseness has been achieved by:

- ridiculously small (and reader unfriendly) margins and font sizes – the point we mentioned earlier
- compressing information to such an extent that nothing of interest is left.

Key point
How to achieve conciseness

Whilst it is true that CVs which are too long do not get read (or do not get read properly), CVs which are too short can just as easily end up on the turn-down pile because they lack detail or say nothing of interest. The message is to achieve conciseness by ensuring the information in your CV is *relevant* to the purpose for which you want to use it.

Warning
Wackiness

Making your CV interesting is not an invitation to unleash the more adventurous or humorous side of your literary talents. Remember, you don't know who will be reading your CV and what you may find hilarious or switched on may come across to someone else as childish or stupid.

What makes a CV interesting?

Broadly speaking, anything in your background that is not standard will be interesting providing – and this is important – it's relevant to the task you want your CV to perform. The reader of your CV is the one you need to focus upon. This is the person who has to find it interesting, no one else.

Notepad
This point about making your CV interesting marries up with a point we make later in the book about using your CV to bring out

your strong points. As we shall see, directing recipients of your CV to what's good about you is especially important when attacking the visible or advertised job market where the competition is going to be tough.

That 'little bit of you'

Going back to our Introduction, we commented that one of the sad things about bland stereotyped CVs is that any trace of individuality (that 'little bit of you') tends to be lost. No one warms to a cardboard cut-out and, sadly, this is the way many people come across in their CVs. There's nothing to hook on to, nothing real, and the engagement factors don't get going for that reason alone.

Don't feel inhibited when you're writing a CV. Use the words and expressions that you would normally use and don't take too much notice of experts who would tell you differently. In particular, don't resort to words and phrases that are not familiar to you and will only serve to convey a completely false impression (for instance, buzz words). At worst, this can lead to a situation at an interview where the person sitting on the other side of the desk is left wondering which is the real you, and whether there is any credibility in anything you're saying.

Questions and answers

CV management

Q *I take the point about the need to tailor CVs to the purpose for which they're intended, but won't this lead to confusion? With so many versions of my CV in circulation will it be hard to keep track of who's received which version?*

A Confusion is only half of it. As we shall show later in the book, the CV you submit in support of an application for a job frequently goes on to set the agenda for any interviews. The interviewer will have your CV on the desk and will proceed to ask questions on the information you've given. On the whole, this dictating of the agenda works greatly in your favour but clearly, before you go to the interview, you need to revisit the CV you submitted and remind yourself what you said in it. Obviously you need to be revisiting the right version of your CV and not one that you sent to someone else. All this adds up to being on the ball with your job applications – a subject we will cover in Chapter 10. Generally, this means building up a dossier of all relevant documents for every application, including a copy of the CV you submitted.

Handwritten CVs

Q *Taking on board all you've said about the importance of that 'little bit of you', it seems at odds to be advising against handwriting CVs. Can you explain this?*

A Rightly or wrongly, handwritten CVs are seen as old-fashioned, and you need to be aware of this. Also, on a purely practical note, you could be asked to e-mail your CV or submit it on disk. This will be a problem for you straightaway if your CV is handwritten.

Having your CV professionally prepared

Q *Bearing in mind the importance of a good CV, isn't it best to go to an expert and have one professionally prepared?*

A A professionally prepared CV is quite easy to spot and, from the recipient's point of view, it tends to beg the question, 'Why can't this candidate put his or her own CV together?' More problematic perhaps is the fact that professionally prepared CVs are among the worst offenders when it comes to blandness and churning out the same tired old descriptions and superlatives again and again. The candidate either does not come across in his or her true light or does not come across at all. There is nothing to latch on to and the engagement factors don't work.

Summary

In this chapter we have looked at the task you face and what you set out to achieve when you sit down to the job of designing a CV. We have seen that:

- no one single CV is going to address all the needs you have
- you need to think in terms of designing your CV individually for the purpose for which it is intended.

We have also seen how CVs occupy a unique place because they are usually the first impression of us received by a prospective employer or by someone else important to our aims in life. We have noted the specialness of first impressions and how, as part of the task of drawing up your CV, you need to make sure your

CV makes the right impression when it arrives at the other end. This impression will play a big part in carrying your CV forward and in making it do the job you want it to do.

Finally we have pointed to the need to do something to lift your CV out of the ordinary and nondescript, and we have suggested two ways in which to do this:

1 Make it interesting (interesting to the reader that is).
2 Put that 'little bit of you' into it.

These two themes will crop up time and time again throughout the book. If the magic is going to work for you in selection or in business or for whatever reason you need your CV, then the person who reads it has got to see something that he or she likes. This won't happen if your CV is boring or stereotyped or lacking in character.

02
making it work for you

In this chapter you will learn:
- how to use your CV to communicate your ambitions
- how to avoid discouragement and time-wasting
- how to connect with the right opportunities
- what is takes to be 'employer-friendly'

The message

A good CV is one that makes it clear to everyone:

- where you're coming from
- what you're seeking to achieve.

Why is this important? The following case study shows what can happen when the recipient of someone's CV picks up the wrong message.

Case study: Kelly

Kelly works in sales for an office equipment supplier. She is 27, good at her job, but dissatisfied with the salary she is paid. She has made her concerns known to her boss, the sales director, on a number of occasions but so far she has received nothing except empty promises.

Feeling she is getting nowhere, Kelly decides to try her luck on the job market and, with this in mind, she turns her attention to updating her CV. Her CV was last updated three years ago when she was applying for her present position, and Kelly is pleased to see that it requires little in the way of attention. Her current job needs to be added to her employment history of course and she has recently moved to a new apartment but, other than that, her CV looks fine and ready to use.

Over the next few weeks, Kelly keeps her eye on the job ads in the local evening newspaper. She picks out a number of sales positions that look interesting and, in each case, she puts an application in the post along with a copy of her CV. She notices that few of the ads she replies to quote a salary. The information given is usually limited to phrases such as 'excellent earnings package' or 'negotiable' or some other similar phrase.

As a result of this activity Kelly gets invited to four interviews. This is where she runs into her first problem because she has to ask for time off work. Unfortunately, she has used all of her holiday entitlement and so she has to invent four different excuses to give to the sales director. The sales director agrees to her requests but Kelly can see that he is suspicious.

At each of the interviews Kelly asks for more information on salary. The interviewers are cagey, however, explaining that salary will be discussed at a later stage.

With one of the jobs, Kelly is invited back for a second interview. She asks the sales director for more time off but on this occasion she is met by a barrage of questions. The sales director wants to know what's going on and makes the comment that Kelly seems to be putting her private life before her work. Thankfully Kelly manages to bluff her way through. Nevertheless, she feels uncomfortable and hopes that she doesn't have to ask for any more time off.

The second interview is with a company which leases vending equipment and it goes well with the interviewer closing the interview by saying she'll get back to Kelly in a couple of days. Sure enough, two days later Kelly gets a call on her mobile to say that the job is hers. Then the part Kelly wasn't expecting – they'll match her salary, and, if conditions are favourable at the end of the year, they'll see what they can do about giving her a rise. What does she think? Kelly isn't sure what to say. She went out onto the job market for more money not a sideways move. Can the vending equipment lease company tweak its offer to make the pay more attractive? Kelly poses the question but the answer she receives is no. Matching her current salary is as far as they are prepared to go. Asking for 24 hours to think over the offer, Kelly realizes that she has already made her mind up. It would be pointless to move for the same money; the right decision is to turn the offer down. What bothers her is the prospect of having to go back to square one and start her job search all over again. As for having more time off work to go to interviews, Kelly is seriously concerned about getting in the sales director's bad books.

Define the aim

The first step in preparing a CV is to be clear about what you want it to do for you. In Kelly's case, she wanted her CV for job hunting but, more specifically, she wanted to find a job where she would be paid more money. How much more? The evidence in the case study suggests that she didn't give enough thought to actual figures. It was only when the vending equipment lease company put its offer on the table that she decided that moving sideways with the vague promise of an increase later on didn't come up to her expectations. Having taken this view she was right to turn the offer down, but proceeding in this way brought two problems in its wake:

1 **Discouragement:** having a number of interviews, getting on a short list and then finding that the job doesn't measure up is,

to say the least, disappointing. However, chalk up a few experiences like this and you will find your disappointment turns into discouragement. You will start to feel there is nothing out there for you and this will cause you either to: (a) lower your sights (lower your ambitions); or (b) give up because you feel you can't take any more. Needless to say, neither is good.

2 **Time-wasting:** time is precious and, in Kelly's case, this manifests itself in the amount of time she can have off work to go to interviews without inviting the suspicions of her boss. As Kelly found, stock excuses like going to the dentist or attending the funeral of some distant aunt can soon start to wear thin. Before she knows it, she will be in the position of having to put her job hunting on hold until, perhaps, she has more holiday entitlement.

Have an aim with a positive outcome

This is important. Too many people define their aims in negative terms. Here are a few examples:

'I'm paid peanuts.'

'I'm in a dead end job.'

'My boss doesn't support me.'

'Having to drive into the city every day is a nightmare.'

'My firm won't pay for me to go on courses.'

True perhaps, but these negative statements do not help us to define the path we want our futures to follow and, ultimately, to define the message we want our CV to deliver.

What would be better? With each of the examples let's turn the negative thought around and see if we can replace it with something more positive.

'I want to earn 2K more in my next job.'

'I'm looking for a job with good prospects for promotion.'

'I want to work for a more professional outfit.'

'I want a job in x, y or z location.'

'I'm looking for an employer who will invest in my development and training.'

Warning

Although you need to send out strong clear messages to readers of your CV, it's important that you say nothing that could lead them into thinking that you're walking around with a chip on your shoulder (a guaranteed way of putting the kiss of death on your applications). Therefore, avoid listing your grumbles and groans. Put everything in a positive context. Focus your thoughts on where you're going next rather than clouding your vision by pondering on the problems attached to what you're doing now.

Take responsibility

Returning to the case study, one school of thought would say that it was the employer's fault that it took two interviews and a phone call to find out that the salary they were offering didn't match up with what Kelly was looking for. They were running the show, after all, and they were the ones who refused to talk about money at the preliminary interview.

However, Kelly is trying to connect her aspirations to the right jobs, and apportionment of blame isn't really the issue. The fact is that she has squandered a valuable part of her available time on a completely fruitless exercise and she is feeling despondent about having to start all over again. Even more worrying perhaps is the prospect that events could repeat themselves – she could go on having interviews with employees who can't afford her. So what's the answer? The answer in fact comes in two parts. The first part is recognizing that the responsibility for communicating the messages about where you're coming from and what you're seeking to achieve rests on you and no one else.

In turn, this means not relying on employers to do the job for you by reading between the lines of your CV or by conducting their selection procedures in what to you would seem to be a more sensible fashion. Some will but some won't and the diversity of the job market is such that you must allow for all situations – including the one Kelly found herself in.

Communicating the message

The second part of the answer is to communicate the message. Once you've taken on board that it's down to you to avoid time-wasting and disappointing mismatches how do you go about it? More importantly, how do you ensure that your applications connect with the right jobs, i.e. the ones that will come up to your expectations?

How employers see it

Employers are just as keen as you are to avoid time-wasting. In the case of Kelly the vending equipment lease company had to count the cost of running a recruiting exercise that had nothing to show at the end of it. This included the cost of:

- advertising
- time spent on interviews
- time spent on administrative tasks such as dealing with applications, invitations to interviews, turning down unsuccessful candidates etc.
- having to operate short-staffed.

The vending machine lease company may have an acceptable number-two choice on the interview list to fall back on, but if they don't, they will be faced with the unappealing prospect of repeating their recruitment exercise (and running up the same costs) all over again.

Get the message across

Going back to Kelly, we saw how she revised a CV that she'd used previously. She brought her employment history up to date and she put in her new address. What she neglected to do, however, was to include in her CV any mention of what she was hoping to achieve by moving jobs, i.e. a significant increase in salary (significant enough to make the move worthwhile). As a result, any prospective employer picking up her CV would not be able to form a view on whether the job she was applying for lined up with her aspirations or not.

> **Key point**
> **Let employers help you**
>
> If employers know what you want out of life, they will be able to see whether that is consistent with what they can offer. If Kelly had made it clear in her CV that she was looking for ?K more on her salary, then there is a good chance that the vending equipment lease company would have picked up the mismatch straight away. Her application would have gone no further or the subject of salary would have come up earlier in the discussions.

What you need to include

The issue that Kelly was seeking to address by shopping around on the job market was one of salary. Put in simple terms, she was looking for more money, and this is the message she needed to get across in her CV. Other people will have different messages. For example, someone who has just been through a succession of jobs that haven't lasted very long and who is looking for secure permanent employment will need to make it clear that another short-term job won't interest them. Similarly, someone on the job market for promotion reasons will need to send out a message to prospective employers setting out the kind of opportunities that are going to be suitable.

The point to messages like these is that they have got to be given prominence in a clear and unambiguous form so that anyone picking up your CV will be in no doubt about what you're looking for in life and, conversely, what you aren't. In this way there will be no room for misunderstandings.

Set out your pay expectations

Irrespective of what you hope to gain by going out on the job market, you need:

- to have clear ideas about what you expect to earn in your next position
- to transmit your pay expectations to prospective employers in your CV.

Money may not be the main reason why you are setting off on your job hunting expedition. It may be, for instance, that you are looking for a promotion opportunity which is not available with your present employer. You want to see what other employers can offer you and your CV will be designed for this purpose. Nevertheless, even though salary isn't the main consideration, you will still need to make it clear to employers what you would view as an acceptable remuneration package so that they will know whether they can afford you or not. Failing to do this will again invite the risk of the wrong messages being picked up. The result could be more time-wasting and discouragement.

Factors to take into account

In determining pay expectations the following factors need to be taken into account:

- what you are earning now
- the market rate for the job in which you see yourself next.

If we go back to the case of Kelly, we saw how she set out to find a job that would pay her more money. She didn't define how much more, but let's say for the sake of argument that she decided that another 2K would be the kind of figure that would make a move worthwhile for her. We now have a target to aim at yet the big question is, 'Is the target attainable?' Are there jobs out there paying the kind of money Kelly is seeking? Or are her pay expectations way over the top and not in tune with the market for people with her level of experience? Conversely, by going after 2K more could she be pitching too low? Could she be in danger of moving from a very badly paid job into one that is still offering way below what someone with her talents could reasonably expect to earn?

Finding out about the market rate

This brings us to one of the major difficulties that faces all job seekers. How do you find out the market rate for someone with your range of skills, knowledge and experience? Where do you go to get this information? How do you know whether the figure you've set your sights on is pitching in too high, too low or somewhere in the middle? Going in too high means you are unlikely to find anything (the salary expectation you flag up in your CV will only put employers off). On the other hand, going in too low could mean that employers queue up to snatch your hand off but you run the risk of selling yourself for less than your proper worth.

In days gone by, the going rate for individual jobs was determined to a large extent by a handful of big firms in a given area. It reflected factors such as:

- the demand in these big firms for people with specified skills
- the big firms' pay bargaining arrangements
- the big firms' internal salary structures.

Today the world is different. Often there are no big firms to dictate the local market rate. Instead, there are dozens and dozens of small- to medium-sized entities who often compete quite ferociously for people. Good news, you may say. Perhaps, but it doesn't make it any easier for people trying to find out whether their pay expectations are consistent with what the market has to offer or not. Added to which is the diversity of the modern market. Towns dominated by one industry have practically disappeared. The steel mill that was once the major provider of jobs has been pulled down and in its place is a business park where high-tech manufacturers sit alongside distribution warehouses, service call centres, mobile phone stockists and the offices of the local environmental health department. What they pay and to whom is largely a mystery. Or at least that's the way it appears.

Where to go for information

In most cases, people go out on to the job market with little or no idea of the kind of salary they can expect to be paid. They proceed with their own notions of what's fair and, not surprisingly, the figure they come up with is often wide of the mark. Given time, people learn from their mistakes. By knocking on countless doors, they find out the hard way that the world isn't prepared to pay them what they feel they're worth. Sadly, however, time can run out on them and they can end up giving up because of what they see as a poor reward for their effort. They throw in the towel because they feel they can't take any more.

How can you avoid this situation? The following are all sources of information from which you can form an overview of whether the salary you're seeking is in line with what the market can offer:

- **Job adverts.** As Kelly noted a lot of ads for jobs don't quote salaries. They use a jumble of words that we're all familiar with such as 'attractive', 'negotiable', 'commensurate with the responsibilities' and so on. Yet there are some ads where salaries do appear. Take into account that employers (or consultants acting on behalf of employers) tend to use salaries in ads where they feel the money on offer is an attractive feature of the job, i.e. the salaries displayed will tend to reflect the upper end of the market range.
- **Consultants.** Because it's their business, recruitment consultants and agencies are a storehouse of information on going rates in particular areas, and you can tap into their knowledge banks simply by paying them a visit. Tell them that you're thinking of looking for another job and ask them to give you an opinion about whether your ideas on salary are realistic or not. Note that consultants who specialize in particular occupational groups will have the best knowledge. For example, a consultancy that specializes in financial appointments will be well placed to advise on salary levels for management accountants, etc.

- **Networking.** Your circle of contacts may be able to provide you with information on what's available 'out there', and often it's simply a case of picking up the phone and asking. Include on your call list people you know who have been active on the job scene recently.

Fine-tuning

From sources such as these you should be able to form an appreciation of what kind of pay is available in your sector of the job market. If your ideas are roughly consistent with the information from your sources, you will know that your targeting isn't too wide of the mark and you can proceed on this basis. The rest is down to fine-tuning – the odd adjustment to your expectations which you may decide to introduce in the light of experience, for instance experience from attending interviews and having to negotiate salaries with employers.

Notepad

One of the questions at the end of this chapter deals with the situation where someone's ideas on pay seem to be way above what the market can offer. See 'Am I asking for too much?', p. 27.

Key point
Flag up your salary expectations

Money is the main reason why most of us go out to work. It is important, therefore, that we use our CVs to flag up where the boundaries of our pay expectations lie in terms of:

- what we're earning now
- what we're looking for in our next job.

We don't want our time wasted by employers who can't afford us. By our omissions we don't want to leave any scope for wrong readings that could lead to the kind of situation Kelly found herself in.

'Employer-friendly'

At the start of Chapter 1 we made the observation that most job seekers see their CVs as having one purpose only and that is to get them interviews. Likewise they view their success in terms of how many of the applications they send off result in interviews.

If they get lots of interviews, they feel that their CV has done a good job for them. What they don't do, however, is count up how many of these interviews are completely pointless exercises because:

- the job doesn't interest them (as in Kelly's case)
- they can't do the job as they are not sufficiently experienced or qualified.

They've wasted another chunk of their precious time off work. They've seen another door close in their face. The damage they are doing to themselves is enormous, and often it's their CV which is at fault for getting them the interview in the first place.

Don't pull the wool over employers' eyes

So far in this chapter we've been looking at the need to use your CV to tell employers what you want out of life. Put your cards on the table and let them decide whether they can meet your aspirations or not. If they can, great, but if they can't then no one wants to see the matter go any further – least of all you.

Similarly, don't use your CV to try to pull the wool over employers' eyes. Embellishing the truth or distorting the facts may help you to get the interview but sooner or later you'll be found out. The interview count may look good but you still have nothing to show at the end of it. Again the danger lies in the time-wasting and the seeds of discouragement that you're sowing.

Key point
Present a true picture

Resist the temptation to use your CV to over-egg your experience and/or qualifications. Always aim to present a true picture of yourself and let employers, with all the facts to hand, make the decision about whether you should be invited to an interview or not. For instance, if there are shortcomings in your experience do not attempt to disguise them or leave them out. Some employers will be happy to live with the shortcomings and some won't. With the first group, you're home and dry. With the second, there's no point in letting the application proceed any further. The sooner it is stopped in its tracks the better.

> **Warning**
>
> It is even worse if you do succeed in pulling the wool over an employer's eyes. For example, a poor interviewer could fall for your deceptions and you could end up in a job that's way beyond your capabilities. The upshot? Stand by for the short, sharp exit treatment, and for the time it's going to take to get your career back on track.

Questions and answers

Tackling employers who are cagey about giving out salary information

Q *I appreciate the difficulty of replying to ads with no information on salary but in the case of someone like Kelly wouldn't it make more sense to ring up before she applies for the job to see what she can find out over the phone?*

A In theory yes, but in practice the evidence of your approach working is rather thin on the ground. Employers who are cagey in ads tend to be equally cagey with cold callers. It may be worth a try, but we still stick to the view that the best way to avoid applications that don't go anywhere is to allow space in your CV for setting out your aspirations, including pay.

Putting your salary in your CV when you're poorly paid

Q *I've been in the same job for the last ten years and am conscious of the fact that I'm very poorly paid compared to people in similar positions with other firms. I have recently decided to do something about my situation by trying my luck on the job market. What bothers me, however, is what to put in my CV about my current earnings. If I tell the truth, employers will see that I am on a low salary and might offer me less than they would offer someone who is being paid a decent wage. Friends have advised me to deal with this problem by re-doing my CV and adding 5K to my salary. My concern with this is that I could get found out because employers have ways and means of finding out people's earnings in previous jobs. What do you think?*

A Your concern is a legitimate one. In the UK, for example, a new employer can check your earnings to date in the tax year by looking at your P45 form. Whether it would alter your new employer's view of you is a different matter. Your question is interesting because it highlights why it is important to include in your CV not just your present salary but also the salary you are looking for. So, don't indulge in worrying deceptions – be up front. Tell the world that just because you're poorly paid now doesn't mean you want to go on being poorly paid. Make it plain to employers that you're not there to be bought on the cheap.

Pay expectations when you're unemployed

Q *My last company where I was employed as a senior manager went into liquidation six months ago and, as a result, I was made redundant with the legal minimum pay-off. I have been trying to find a job on a comparable salary but so far I have had no joy whatsoever and I am now at the point where I will have to take anything that I can get simply because of financial pressures. In hindsight, I feel that I made a mistake by writing in my CV that I was looking for a job on such a high salary. Is the lesson of my experience that the unemployed can't really afford the luxury of having pay expectations?*

A The lesson is that finding the right job with the right salary sometimes takes time and, when you're out of work with financial pressures bearing down on you, time is not on your side. However, you also need to consider that your lack of success with your job applications may have nothing to do with your salary expectations. Other factors may be at play like, for example, a shortage of jobs for people with your range of skills, qualifications and expertise. Situations like these are notoriously difficult to read. Would it help to remove any reference to salary expectations from your CV? We would say no – providing that you have followed the advice in this chapter to ensure as far as you can that your ideas are in line with market rates. What may be more helpful to you, and to anyone else who has the hard luck to find themselves in your situation, is to broaden out your job applications so that you're exploring a number of different avenues at the same time rather than just one. For instance, if your core skills are in accountancy, you could run job applications for accountancy positions alongside your senior management applications. You would quote a salary expectation appropriate to each position, i.e. a different figure depending on the type of job you are applying for. This approach is known as multiple-targeting, and a more detailed explanation can be found in *Teach Yourself Managing Your Own Career* (see Chapter 6, 'When your job is at risk').

Am I asking for too much?

Q *Basically my situation is similar to Kelly's except in my case I've applied for a number of positions where I've got on the shortlist and then been told that the maximum pay on offer is little improvement on what I'm getting in my present job. OK, so I admit I'm guilty of not flagging up my salary expectations in my CV but, if I had, the result would presumably have been no interviews. What do I learn from this? Am I asking for too much? If so, where do I go from here?*

A Are you asking for too much? You will only find the answer to this by researching your niche area of the job market along the lines suggested in this chapter and by listening to the feedback from your experience of making applications. However, with the latter be careful about how you view the feedback because your experience in the shape of interviews with employers who can't match your aspirations may not be typical of the market as a whole. You may be seeing a narrow range of employers and not necessarily the best payers. Let's say though that all the information coming back to you points to your expectations being on the high side. What do you do about it? What do you do when you don't get any interviews and you feel pay could be the reason? Effectively you have three choices:

1 Adjust your expectations down a notch or two (change your CV and see if you get more interviews).
2 Stop applying for jobs.
3 Keep going but with the knowledge that you're targeting a small number of jobs at the top end of the market.

With item 3, the diversity of the modern job market means that there is a surprisingly wide spread of salaries available so, even if your expectations are on the high side, there is still a chance you could find something. The message is to 'keep going'.

What to read into turn-downs

Q *Having gone through a number of experiences like Kelly's, I followed your advice and made it clear in my CV that I would only be interested in a job that paid over ... (I named a fairly high salary level). Sure enough the time-wasting interviews stopped but now all I get is a procession of 'Sorry but no thank you' letters and, in terms of discouragement, I am not sure which is worse. Do you have any comments?*

A We take the point that not many employers will be forthright enough to write back and say that they can't afford you. A far more likely outcome is a standard rejection letter with no reasons given (as your experience bears out). Any comments? Only to agree that turn-down letters can be a source of discouragement if you let them be. It's important to remind yourself that, with any job application, the reason for not getting on the interview list is often a reflection on the job rather than on you. If employers see you as too good, over-qualified, over-ambitious or too highly paid then that's their problem, not yours. Remember this the next time a 'No thank you' letter drops on the doormat.

Summary

The modern job market is a difficult place where people can spend years thrashing around aimlessly and achieving very little. Part of the reason for this aimlessness is a failure on their part to transmit messages about themselves and their ambitions:

- to the market they're trying to tap into
- in terms that the market will understand.

It is rather like running a shop where the goods in the window are under cover and no one's too sure what you're selling. The wrong customers come in and some of them don't have enough money to buy the goods, but who's to blame except you?

The message here is to let everyone know what you want out of life and to use your CV as the vehicle for this transparency. At the same time, view employers as people who will help you if you give them the chance. Make your CV work for you. Make it deliver what you want it to deliver and not something that disappoints, wastes your time or otherwise falls short of expectations.

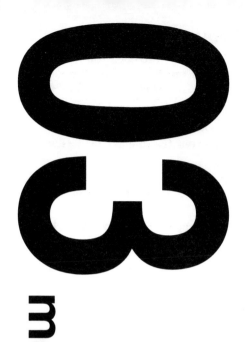

03

making a start

In this chapter you will learn:
- how to put together the framework of your CV
- what to say about yourself
- what to leave out
- the importance of being there to take the calls

The structure of your CV

The first two chapters of this book have provided you with a set of ground rules to follow as you make a start on the job of preparing your CV. To summarize, the ground rules are:

- your CV needs to fit the task for which you intend to use it
- your CV has to convey a good impression of you
- there has got to be enough in your CV to make readers want to engage further with you
- your CV has to be concise and relevant
- your CV has to make it clear to everyone where you're coming from and what you are seeking to achieve.

These ground rules are important and we will keep coming back to them.

Put the framework in place

Your first task is to put the framework of your CV in place. The framework consists of information that won't change (or won't change greatly) from one job application to the next.

When you need a CV, you usually find that you need one quickly – for example, when you need to send off an application for a great job you've seen advertised in the paper. Hence, it is useful to have the framework already prepared so that any work you have to do on it is minimal.

What you need

Most people today own or have access to a PC with one of the standard word-processing packages already installed. A good quality inkjet or laser printer is essential. It will ensure that anything you produce:

- looks good
- is a true reflection of you
- makes the best first impression.

Warning
Using obsolete or worn-out equipment to produce a CV is asking for trouble. Apart from the appearance of the finished product, something that looks like it dates from the age of the ark doesn't do much for your image. So, even though you may be very proud of the old typewriter you've had at home for years, don't use it to

produce your CV. You could send out a signal to readers that you're someone who is stuck in his or her ways and potentially resistant to change, i.e. a bad impression. Take special note if you are over 45. Coming across as a dinosaur is not what you want.

Get set up

With good presentation and making favourable impressions high on the agenda, it might help you to go through the following checklist before you start keying in your information:

• use a conventional font and font size, e.g. Arial 11
• use either bold or underlining to pick out headings – not both
• use the default setting on your software for margins – don't make margins narrower in an effort to get more on the page
• don't use block capitals to highlight words
• be consistent with the number of line spaces you leave between sections (two is fine).

Notepad
Putting the framework of your CV into a word-processed document using conventional PC software and storing it on CD or floppy disk has a number of advantages. It enables you to:

• update your CV (e.g. to add on new qualifications)
• customize your CV to fit the task for which you want to use it
• e-mail your CV
• print off fresh copies as and when you need them.

Keep it concise

This is a reminder that one of the biggest challenges you face when it comes to designing a CV is to keep it concise. Remember the point we made in Chapter 1 about conciseness and the best way to achieve it. Stick to information that is relevant.

Notepad
There is a question at the end of this chapter that deals with the maximum number of pages you can have in a CV without impairing its chances of being read. See 'When is a CV too long?', p. 46.

Get the good bits in at the beginning

A point to note about CVs is that they don't always get read from start to finish. There is a switch-off point part-way through and a good candidate can find themselves on the reject pile simply because they left the best parts till last. Here is an example:

Curriculum Vitae   Page 1

Name	John Ernest Potts
Address	Acacia Bungalow
	Promenade Avenue
	Sunnytown on Sea
	Somerset
	SS99 9SS
e-mail	John-potts@xxxxxxxxxx
Phone	xxxx xxxxxx (home)
	xxxxx xxxxxx (mobile)
Date of birth	12.04.1964
Marital status	Married with two children (16 and 12)
Driving licence	Clean
Health	Good (non-smoker)

Education/Qualifications

1969–1976	Sunnytown on Sea County Primary School
1976–1981	Watery Downs Comprehensive School
Examinations passed:	CSE (Grade One): Science, Metalwork, Engineering Drawing, Mathematics; CSE (Grade Two): English; CSE (Grade Three): French, Religious Education, Geography
1981–1984	Grey Cliff College of Further Education
Examinations passed:	City and Guilds Mechanical Engineering Parts I and II

John Potts is a fictional applicant for a sales manager position with a company in the agrichemicals industry and we are looking at the first page of his CV. What do we learn from this? We see he's living in a nice-sounding place in the West Country. We know his age. We know he has no health problems, doesn't smoke and drives his car carefully. From his schooling we can pick out that he's lived in the same area for much of his life. He left secondary education with average academic achievements and went on, so it seems, to do some kind of engineering apprenticeship, but so what? Who is really interested in half of this information and, more to the point, what is there here that tells us that John Potts is a red hot candidate for the job of sales manager? What grabs our attention and yells at us to turn over and read the next page? The short answer is nothing much.

Key point
Produce a good front page

In a competitive job situation, your CV could be one among hundreds received. There is a need to hit readers in the eye straightaway with what's good about your application, and where better to do it than on the front page of your CV? Similarly, if you are cold-canvassing employers to find out if they have any suitable openings, you need to take into account that they receive dozens of unsolicited CVs – most of them from people who are completely unsuitable. Therefore, you need to use your front page to tell your readers what will interest them most.

This contrasts with filling the front page of your CV with information that, whilst interesting, may not be top of the list when it comes to proclaiming your suitability for a position. For example, in the case of John Potts the information about his school and college qualifications is not likely to figure too prominently in the agrichemicals company's assessment of whether he's the right person to be their next sales manager or not. The information can be relegated to elsewhere in his CV or left out altogether.

Decide the order of information

Consistent with the need for a good first page, present the information in your CV in the order that you think readers will find most interesting. With the exception of first jobbers and career changers where the focus of interest will be on education and motivation respectively, most employers will have their minds fixed firmly on what candidates can offer in terms of their personal attributes and work experience. In the case of John Potts let's say he has managed sales teams in the agrichemicals industry before. This is the information he needs to put at the beginning of his CV, and preferably on the front page.

Number your pages

You can do this by entering the page number as a header or footer – or by doing as John Potts did and simply typing 'Page 1' at the top of the first page and consecutively numbering any continuation sheets.

Why is it important to number your pages? For the simple reason that CVs get faxed and e-mailed, and the person putting them together at the other end needs to know what order the pages go in. Moreover, CVs sent in the post may be stapled together but they can still come apart and the problem of putting them back together in the right order arises again. Simple though they may sound, disciplines like these ensure that your CV is read in the way you want it to be read. It keeps you in control of what is going on when you can't be there in person.

Putting your name on each page

To ensure that your CV doesn't get mixed up with someone else's, make sure your name is on each page, for example, write at the top 'John Potts CV: Page 2' and so on.

What to put in

A reminder that at this stage you are putting together a framework rather than a finished version of your CV that other eyes will see. Where do you begin?

Name

Use the forename by which you are normally known, for example, Steve Smith, Tricia Jones, etc. Put any letters after your name that are relevant: Wendy Green M.Sc., C.Eng. This is a way of telling readers at a quick glance that you're qualified.

Address

Put this in full, including the postcode.

Telephone points of contact

Most contact with the job applicant is over the phone, so telephone numbers are important. The general idea is this: an employer reads your CV, likes what he or she sees then picks up the phone to ask you in for an interview. Fine if you answer, but if you don't (if you're not there or the number is constantly engaged) then this is where the problems start.

Warning

Employers don't waste time on people who are hard to contact – especially when there are plenty of other candidates to choose from.

Telephone points of contact normally include:

- your home phone number
- the number you can be contacted on at work
- the number of your mobile.

Notepad

Listing your telephone points of contact on your CV sounds a simple enough exercise. However, before doing it, you need to go one step further and check that someone using the numbers you've given will actually be able to get through to you. The subject of telephone availability and being there to take the calls is so important that we will return to it again later in this chapter. Note that making it easy for anyone trying to get hold of you is a key part of your employer-friendliness.

E-mail address

E-mail is the way in which most people in business communicate with one another, and so you can enhance your employer friendliness even further by including an e-mail address in your CV. More important still is having the capacity and self-discipline to check your e-mails regularly. Anyone who sends you an e-mail will be expecting to hear back from you quickly and, if they don't, there is an immediate question mark over how you see your priorities and your sense of urgency, i.e. a bad first impression.

Where privacy is an issue, putting a work e-mail address in your CV may not be a good idea.

Date of birth

Many books on CVs advise you to leave out your date of birth because, in these enlightened times, age is not supposed to be a factor that employers take into account. In particular, the advice is aimed at those who might consider their age to be a disadvantage, for instance, the over-50s.

What do we think? Like it or not, leaving out your date of birth can send out a signal that *you* see your age as a problem and, for this reason alone, our advice is don't omit it. Besides, a good CV is there to connect you with the right opportunities and, in this context, what worse scenario can you imagine for someone in their middle years than ending up in an interview with an employer who has no time for anyone over 30? In short, inserting your date of birth is part of the openness and transparency with which you will be engaging the job market.

Key achievements

Picking out the high spots in your career is a good way to quickly focus readers of your CV upon what marks you out as a candidate to be taken seriously. Here, however, we hit a difficulty because what you see as your key achievements may not always be relevant to the purpose for which you intend to use your CV. For example, you may have spent five years running a multi-million dollar construction project in the Middle East, but this won't carry much weight with an employer who is looking for someone to manage a small precision engineering business. Indeed, going into raptures about the work you did overseas could send out the message that this is where you would rather be, i.e. running a small precision engineering business is something you view as a stop-gap. This would be a reason to reject your application.

The bottom line is that the key achievements section of your CV is something you should leave blank at this stage. When you come to fill it in, you will be highlighting areas of experience that connect directly with what the reader of your CV will be looking for. There will be much more about this in Chapters 4–9 where we will look at designing CVs for specific purposes.

Warning

A common fault of CVs is when people list too many 'key achievements' so that:

- the impact is lost
- very little of what is listed is relevant
- the achievements aren't really achievements.

See your key achievements section as the opportunity to tell your readers about what makes you special. With this in mind, keep the list to about four or five bullet points and view any more as disposable (get ready to start editing). At the same time, stick to the facts and avoid self-eulogies. You may think that you're the best thing since sliced bread but saying so in your CV won't help you and could turn some readers off.

Employment history

List the organizations you've worked for, the positions you've held, and a summary of your main responsibilities with the dates. Also include your reason for leaving. Remember 'career advancement' is going to sound better than 'couldn't get on with the CEO'. If you are currently unemployed, say so.

Place your jobs in reverse order, putting your present or most recent position first. Why? Because what you're doing now (or what you did last) is likely to be of more interest to readers of your CV than what you did at the start of your career. Remember the point about having the best parts of your CV at the beginning and preferably on the front page.

Education

List the schools and colleges you've attended together with the dates.

Qualifications

List the examinations you've passed together with dates and grades. Include any current courses of study with the envisaged completion dates.

Training courses

List any training courses you've attended (ones that are relevant) together with the dates and the name of the course organizer.

Languages/Information Technology skills

Where the information is relevant, give details of your level of proficiency.

Ambitions

Consistent with the lessons in Chapter 2, tell readers of your CV what you're looking for in life – with sufficient clarity to avoid misunderstandings. Do this in three sentences maximum. For example, 'Due to the relocation of my company I am currently commuting over 100 miles a day. I am seeking a position in purchasing in the Nottingham/Derby areas. My current salary is XX p.a. and I am looking for something similar.'

Note that if you are pursuing a number of different career ambitions, it may be better to leave this section blank in the framework version of your CV.

Salary

In cases like the example above, salary can be covered in 'Ambitions'. Otherwise, give details of your current or most recent salary including any significant perks such as company cars, medical plans, share options, etc. State clearly what you're looking for in your next job.

Personal statement

In certain situations it will help to give more information about yourself. For instance, if you are contemplating a complete change of career and your CV is being designed for this purpose, it will help to explain why you have decided to seek fresh fields.

Period of notice

Prospective employers will want to know how quickly you can join them. If you're unemployed you can say that you can start immediately.

Medical history

Give details in plain English of any medical conditions, including disabilities, that might have a bearing on your ability to do the job for which you are applying. Indicate any special needs, for example, wheelchair access, specialized VDU equipment, etc. If you have no medical history, say so and remember that no one will be interested to hear about the dose of chickenpox you had when you were in primary school. If you are a non-smoker include this information in your CV (it carries weight in the eyes of some employers).

Nationality

British, Norwegian, Australian – put your nationality in your CV. Where relevant, include information on residential status, work permits, etc. Employers need to know that they won't have any hassle from the authorities if they take you on.

Marital status

Single, divorced, married with two children – keep it simple.

Leisure time activities

Again, keep it short and simple. Long lists of leisure activities can give the impression of not being very work-oriented. Leave out any strange hobbies. The same goes for sports where injuries could be a feature (and be a cause of absence from work).

References

Give the names, addresses and daytime telephone numbers of two referees. Ideally one of these referees will have first-hand knowledge of your work (e.g. an ex-boss). The other will be someone who knows you personally and will be able to vouch for your character. Get permission before you use anyone's name as a referee (this is important).

Notepad
Again, a reminder that here we are producing a framework CV –
something you can work on and adapt as and when the need for
a CV arises.

See the Appendix (p. 135) for an example of a framework CV.

Telephone availability

We said we would return to this subject and here we are! The
issue, you remember, is ensuring that recipients of your CV can
get hold of you easily and quickly by using the telephone
numbers you have given.

Most interviews are fixed up over the phone and so an
important part of getting you to interviews is to make sure you
can take the calls. Easy? It sounds it, but, pause for a few
moments to consider your telephone availability and how good
it is.

How interview lists are decided

Example: XYZ Company
Halfway through the seasonal peak, XYZ Company loses one of
its area account executives to a competitor. In the short term –
and to stall any loss of business until a suitable replacement can
be found – Pippa, XYZ's sales manager, takes over the vacant
territory herself. This, she realizes, can't be allowed to go on for
too long because of the conflicting demands on her time. In fact,
getting the vacancy filled as quickly as she can is her only way to
keep the competition at bay and take some of the pressure off
herself.

Pippa receives just over 40 replies to the various ads she places
in newspapers and trade journals. She takes the bundle home
with her one evening, figuring she'll have more chance of some
peace and quiet within her own four walls.

Pippa starts the task of drawing up an interview list by dividing
the applicants into two piles: those who look interesting, and
those who don't. Having done this, she goes through the
interesting pile a second time picking out eight candidates who,
from an experience point of view, look particularly promising.

These, she decides, are the ones she is going to see and, with her diary at the ready, she proceeds to ring each of them. By now it is 8.30 p.m.

Seven out of Pippa's eight selected candidates have thought to put their home phone numbers in their CVs. Five of these she manages to contact straightaway, and suitable times and dates for interviews are fixed. With the remaining two:

• one is a number which rings out (no one answers)
• the other is constantly engaged.

Pippa thinks through her options. She could try the candidates she hasn't managed to contact another time – or alternatively she could write to them and ask them to phone in. On the other hand, five candidates seem plenty to choose from bearing in mind that she is in a hurry to get the vacant slot filled as quickly as she can. No, she decides finally, she'll stick with the five interviews she's fixed up already and go back to the others if she has to (if none of the five prove to be suitable).

Points to pick out

• Managers like Pippa who don't have time on their side move quickly when it comes to setting up interviews.
• They use the phone to make contact with the candidates they want to see.
• The calls can come at any time – evenings are a particularly good time for catching people at home (where they will be away from office eavesdroppers and able to speak more freely).
• Employers don't waste time on people they find hard to contact – especially when there are plenty of other candidates to choose from.
• In situations like this, telephone availability plays a big part in determining whether you get on the interview list or not.

Other factors you need to appreciate

Advances in telecommunications technology, and the fact that we are living in an increasingly paperless world mean that not just managers in a hurry like Pippa resort to contacting candidates by phone. Furthermore, managers are not surrounded by armies of secretaries anymore so, when it comes to getting a letter out, they're usually faced with the task of having to do it themselves. Small wonder, therefore, that they choose to take the easy route and ring the candidates.

Consultants

Consultants are another reason why contact with candidates is more often by phone. Consultants are involved in an ever-increasing number of recruitment situations. Consultants are habitual users of the phone; they rarely communicate by any other means.

Notepad

'Why didn't I get picked for an interview?' is the question every unsuccessful candidate asks. 'Why didn't they ask to see me when I've got all the qualifications for the job?'

The answer in many cases is very simple: these candidates weren't there to take the calls. Of course, the 'Dear John' letter they received didn't tell them that.

Telephone interviews

This is a trend of recent years. What happens is as follows. You apply for a job you see advertised by sending in your CV then, to your surprise, you get a phone call from someone you've never heard of before asking if it's a convenient moment to run through a few questions with you. Telephone interviews are yet another good reason why telephone availability is crucial.

Recruiters with a long list of telephone interviews to carry out will persist to a point and try to make contact with candidates but, if their efforts are repeatedly frustrated by phones that aren't answered or phones that are constantly engaged, sooner or later they say to themselves, 'Enough is enough'.

Key point
Telephone availability

With so much competition in the job market the first task you face (always) is to get your name on the interview list. Good telephone availability is a valuable asset to have on your side.

Telephone numbers in your CV

As part of your employer-friendliness, list your telephone points of contact in your CV. To remind you, telephone points of contact mean:

* your home phone number
* the number you can be contacted on at work
* the number of your mobile.

Let's look at each of these in turn.

Your home phone number

As we have seen, phoning candidates in the evening when they get home from work is favoured by many recruiters because it provides the facility to talk freely. Ways to make yourself more employer-friendly include:

* giving in your CV a rough idea of the time you normally get home, for example, 'after 6.30 p.m.' inserted alongside your home phone number
* considering any routine ins and outs – for example, if you are routinely out on Tuesdays and Thursdays because you play squash and attend an evening class, make sure you mention this.

Work numbers

Consider whether your name would be instantly recognized by whoever answers the phone in your organization, e.g. the receptionist. If not, it may be necessary to insert an extension number in your CV – or the name of the department where you work.

Mobile phones

On the face of it mobile phones provide the perfect answer to telephone availability, and recruiters are increasingly disposed towards ringing people on their mobiles. Any snags? Only if your mobile is switched off for long periods because of your job or if you are regularly in areas where signal strength is poor. The answer here is to make sure that you have a message-taking facility and, more importantly, that you check your messages regularly. Take it from us, people who don't return their messages are a recruiters' nightmare. Also, if you return a call late you may find that all the interviews are already booked up.

Notepad

By giving a choice of home-work-mobile phone numbers you are giving employers more than one route to getting to you. This is important where people like managers and consultants are working to tight time scales and where the need to get you in for an interview may be urgent.

Test your home telephone availability

Here is an interesting exercise for you to try out. Put yourself in the position of someone trying to get hold of you. You've given your home phone number in your CV, and you have said that you're normally in after 6.30 p.m. Put this to the test over, say, a two-week period. Employers on the whole will take you literally. They will phone you at 6.30 p.m. and, if they fail to get through for any reason, they may try again ten minutes later. Monitor what would happen if someone tried ringing you at 6.30 p.m. and 6.40 p.m. on the dot each evening Monday to Friday.

• Would you be in?
• Would anyone be in?
• Most importantly, how many times would the number ring out engaged?

The aim of this exercise is to expose flaws in your availability – flaws that will probably surprise you – like:

• the number of times you're late
• the number of times you pick up the phone the minute you walk through the door
• how often other people in the family are on the phone or using the line to access the internet.

An availability audit such as this is intended to throw up points for action. These could include:

• Whether 6.30 p.m. is a bit ambitious. Whether saying 7.00 p.m. would be better (just to be on the safe side).
• Whether you need to introduce some disciplines at home during periods when you're applying for jobs, e.g. no blocking the line between 6.30 p.m. and 7.30 p.m. in the evenings.

- Whether you need a call-waiting bleep or some other facility to alert you to the fact that someone is trying to get through.
- Whether you need to go the whole hog and install a second line (one for your use only).
- Whether you need a message-taking facility.
- Whether you need to invest in more advanced telephone technology, e.g. a call-minding system linked to your mobile phone.

Availability aids

The amount of telecommunications gadgetry on the market has mushroomed in recent years. Consequently, the question facing many people is how much they need to spend on availability aids.

If you have a normal nine to five job and you're at home most weekday evenings, you shouldn't present too many challenges to someone trying to get hold of you. On the other hand, if you work irregular hours and/or your job involves nights away from home, investment in technology may be the right thing for you. The answer to the question, therefore, depends on your lifestyle.

Warning

If your investment in gadgetry includes any kind of message-taking facility, make sure you check your messages systematically and regularly. For example, when you arrive back from work, make it your first job to check any messages that may have been left on your answer phone (employers are especially unforgiving to people who fail to return their calls promptly).

If your work takes you away from home you will need the facility to access your messages remotely.

Key point

Engage the job market with what it wants – good candidates who are trouble-free to deal with.

Questions and answers

When is a CV too long?

Q *Is it right that a CV should be three pages of A4 maximum? If my CV is any longer will it reduce the chances of it being read?*

A Not if it's interesting. However, the point is that CVs longer than three pages of A4 often aren't read fully because a fair proportion of the information they contain isn't relevant. You need to apply this test of relevance to what you decide to include. If you do, you will find that the length of your CV takes care of itself.

Office telephone numbers and concerns about confidentiality

Q *I don't want anyone to find out that I'm looking for another job and for this reason I don't want phone calls at the office. Is it best therefore to leave my work telephone number out of my CV?*

A It won't put off a determined recruiter (he or she will simply look up the number of your firm in the book). What might work better for you is to put 'with discretion' after your work number. In this way most people will get the message but if you do get an insistent caller and the ears around you are flapping, all you need to say is, 'Can I ring you back later please?' – and make the call in surroundings more conducive to private conversations.

Not revealing your employer's identity

Q *Rather like your last questioner I would not want it to get out that I'm looking for another job, and for this reason I haven't included the name of my present employer in my CV. Any comment?*

A In most cases, the fear you are voicing is unfounded (recipients of your CV will respect the confidentiality of the information you have given). However, if you do feel uncomfortable about revealing your employer's name in a document that is going to go into general circulation then don't do it. Any downsides? Yes, where your track record with a particular employer would mark you out as a leading contender for a position (e.g. a brand leader).

Photographs

Q *Is it a good idea to include a photograph of myself in my CV?*

A We must confess to mixed feelings. On the one hand, putting a face to a name seems like a good idea and a way of getting the engagement factors working. On the other, CVs get faxed and photocopied as part of their processing and, as a result, photographs can end up looking very unflattering. Advice? Unless you are particularly photogenic, give it a miss.

Leaving jobs off your CV

Q *I worked for a company for over 15 years but recently I have had a lot of jobs including some where I was given the sack. Frankly I found it hard to settle after so long with one employer. I realize this won't look good on my CV so should I leave some of the jobs out?*

A We understand the difficulty of finding it hard to settle, but the trouble with what you are suggesting is that you will be giving prospective employers information that is incorrect. Where this becomes tricky is if you take a job then at some point in the future your new employer finds out that you worked at a company that wasn't included in your CV. How will they react to this information? It depends on the employer and, let's face it, much will depend on how you've proved yourself in the job by then. On the whole, we feel you would be much happier proceeding into the future without any skeletons rattling around in the cupboard. List out your succession of jobs. Employers, particularly the better ones, don't expect people to be perfect but they do expect them to be honest.

Summary

We live in a fast-moving world where we frequently have to react quickly to situations and opportunities. This is why it is important to have a framework CV in place. You won't be faced with having to start from scratch and end up doing a rush job. You will be able to focus your attention on gilding the lily and adding the fine detail that will enable your CV to deliver the result you are seeking. Chapters 4–9 will help you to tailor your CV depending upon the purpose for which you need it.

04

CVs for attacking the competition

In this chapter you will learn:

- how to make your CV stand out from the rest
- how to engage and overcome competition
- what it takes to get picked for interviews

Cracking tough job markets

Good jobs attract large numbers of applicants. Exactly how many tends to be determined by:

- how good is good
- how widely the job has been advertised.

In Chapter 1 we gave the example of Anji (Example A). Anji was a sales high-flyer in the telecommunications industry who was seeking to maximize her earnings by going after top paid jobs which she saw advertised in national newspapers or on the websites of leading companies. The main task she faced was one of engaging and overcoming competition. She was going to be up against many other equally well-qualified applicants, and getting on the interview list wouldn't be easy. Somehow, she had to make her application stand out from the crowd, and this was the task her CV had to perform for her.

Key point
Address competition

When the competition is hot, it is no use sending in the standard version of your CV – it will simply get buried with the rest. Something special is needed, something that will grab the reader's attention and make them sit up and take notice of you.

How interview lists are decided

To give you a flavour of the challenge you face when you design a CV aimed at seeing off competition, let's consider what happens when employers receive large numbers of applications for positions they have advertised.

Where processing huge responses is a regular occurrence, preliminary scanning of CVs may be done by computer (there will be more on this subject later in this chapter). Otherwise, the task of sifting through CVs will fall on a manager rather like it fell on Pippa in the example of XYZ company in Chapter 3.

How they proceed with this task is very much down to the individual, but most will do as Pippa did and start by giving the CVs they have received a preliminary scan before deciding which candidates to bring in for an interview. It is worth noting that:

- managers have many conflicting demands on their time
- the more CVs there are, the less time will be given to reading each one
- 'reading' may consist of little more than a quick glance focused on picking out key points of interest (key to the reader, that is)
- CVs are not always read from start to finish (the point we noted in Chapter 3)
- CVs are rarely read twice (once on the turn-down pile, they tend to stay there).

The one-quick-read test

What this means in competitive job situations is that:

- what you have to offer has got to come across in one quick read of your CV because it won't get another chance
- what you have to offer has to match up with what the employer wants, and this has to come across straightaway.

Selection criteria

So what are employers looking for? If the competition is fierce, which of your attributes will be the most compelling when it comes to booking your place on the interview list?

Employers are not all the same

When putting together a CV, one of the biggest mistakes you can make is to view all employers as the same. Take two companies advertising positions in human resources management. Company A is highly unionized where practically everything is determined by collective bargaining. Company B, on the other hand, is a traditional paternalistic employer where there is very little trade union involvement, and the main function of human resources management is administering the company's welfare and benefits schemes.

A candidate advertising a track record as a hard-nosed negotiator would carry considerable clout with Company A, whereas this would be of little interest to Company B. Indeed, it might even put them off.

Looking for clues to employers' thinking

So, given this diversity, how do you find out about the qualities that employers are seeking in people? Out of your list of attributes, how do you know which ones will interest them and which ones won't?

Clues in advertisements

If you saw the job advertised in a newspaper or journal, or on a website, the first place to look is in the ad itself. 'The ideal candidate will have ...', 'This position calls for someone with ...'. Here you have employers telling you want they what to see. The message? Read ads carefully (few candidates do).

Notepad
Picking up clues to employers' thinking from advertisements is not simply a matter of taking in the obvious. There are often other clues to be picked up from reading between the lines. For example, we recently saw an ad for a projects manager that talked extensively about the company's overseas customer base. The coded message here was that having no qualms about going off for long periods and living out of a suitcase was one of the criteria that would be used to assess candidates.

Tap into your networks

We move in small worlds, and it is likely that someone among your circle of contacts has some inside information on the employer that interests you. Tap into this information and see what you can find out. Note that people who have made applications previously can be very useful sources of information on what employers view as important. Make a point of picking the brains of anyone you know who has been active on the job market recently.

Search the internet

Finding out what you can about an employer from the internet is a quick and easy way of sourcing information. For instance, you will be able to find out more about what a company does from its website. You may even be able to get some insight into its culture, and again this will help you to form an appreciation of what qualities they value in people.

Inspired guesswork

From the information you accumulate from these sources, you may be able to make a few inspired guesses about what desirable attributes the employer is looking for. Don't hesitate to do this. To illustrate, a company that operates in a tightly-knit industry will have a natural predisposition towards candidates who have experience in the same trade, even though they won't mention this in their advertisement.

Warning

Whilst it is important to find out what you can about employers' selection criteria, it should never become a reason for delay. With highly visible (advertised) jobs that are going to attract fierce competition it is crucial to submit your application as quickly as possible. Remember, there will be no brownie points for producing the best CV ever to then find out it has arrived too late. There will be more about getting a move on with your applications later in this chapter.

Give prominence to your strong points

Remember that this chapter is about producing a CV that engages and overcomes competition. Therefore, let's focus our thoughts on what is good about your application. What are your strong points?

Finding the matches

How do you define a strong point? Simply, it is where there is a match between what you have to offer and what the employer is seeking (the selection criteria).

Strong points could include any of the following:

- you hold the right qualifications
- you have the right kind of experience
- you have received a particular type of training
- you have the kind of personal qualities the employer is looking for
- you live in the right place.

Key point

Strong points in this context mean strong points vis-à-vis a particular job application, and this may not be the same as your general strong points. For example, you may have had a lot of interesting experience in designing applications for a particular brand of computer software but this won't cut much ice with an employer who uses completely different systems.

Make your strong points count

Don't worry if you haven't got all the attributes an employer wants – what is important at this stage is that:

- you identify the attributes that you do have
- you emphasize your strong points in the design of the CV that you are going to submit.

Your key achievements

You will remember that we left this section blank when we put together the framework version of your CV in Chapter 3. This was so that you had a place where you could summarize the strong points on the front page of your CV. Write a list of bullet points that highlights why you are a red hot candidate for this position, and then count up how many you have. Are there more than six? If the answer is yes, go through the list again because you're probably including achievements that:

- aren't really strong points
- won't have any impact on your application
- need to be taken out.

Remember that:

- you're up against competition
- the reader may have looked at 60 CVs before yours
- you want the reader to turn over to the next page
- you need to focus the reader's attention quickly on what's good about you
- to ensure their prominence, your strong points need to stand out.

Warning

With listing key achievements avoid slipping into toe-curling self-eulogies because people who look at CVs have seen it all before and won't be impressed.

Backing up your strong points

Having listed your strong points under your key achievements on the front page of your CV, you then need to back up the information in the detail that follows. For instance, imagine that you're applying for a job as a designer with a cutting-edge design company. One of the desirable candidate attributes listed in the advertisement is familiarity with a less well-known computer-aided design package. Let's say that you happen to have experience of using this package with a previous employer – you need to identify the experience as one of the strong points in your application and list it in your key achievements. You should also back up this information by expanding upon the job with the previous employer in the employment history section of your CV. In other words, bring your experience with the package into greater prominence by affording more space to your time with this particular previous employer than you would have done with any other application.

Notepad

Bringing your strong points into prominence needs to be consistent with keeping your CV short and concise. To achieve this, you may have to take out some cherished piece of information to make the necessary space. Console yourself with the fact that the strong point will have more bearing on whether you get picked for an interview or not. In competitive situations, this is all that matters.

Use their words

The choice of words is important in CVs designed to engage and overcome competition. Therefore, use their words – by which we mean put your own preferences to one side and use the same jargon and buzz words that employers use in their ads. Employers hear echoes of their own thinking if you use their words. It gets your strong points across immediately, whereas your choice of words may not have the same impact.

Accompanying letters

When you mail a CV to an employer, you will put an accompanying letter with it and this gives you yet another opportunity to set out your strong points. Here is some guidance on how to produce a good accompanying letter:

• Bearing in mind that employers may have more than one vacancy at any given point in time, make it clear which position you are applying for by reference to the job title and, if relevant, the newspaper or journal where you saw it advertised.

• Say why you feel you meet the criteria for the job by listing your strong points, i.e. the same information that you've put in the key achievements section of your CV (don't worry about repeating it).

• Tell the employer how to get hold of you (your telephone and e-mail points of contact – again don't worry about giving the same information twice).

• Keep the letter short and to the point (one sheet of A4 if possible).

Here is an example of a letter of application:

18 Marigold Gardens, Anytown, AT99 9XX

17 January 20XX

Mr B. Fisher
Chief Accountant
Nifty Nimble Dietary Products Limited
Othertown
OT99 9ZZ

Dear Mr Fisher

Credit Manager

I wish to apply for the position advertised in tonight's *Evening Bugle*. A copy of my CV is enclosed.

Please note that:

- I have ten years' experience on sales ledger and credit control work including the last three in a management position in which I am responsible for five staff
- I have worked with manual and computerized systems
- I am fully mobile and hold a clean driving licence
- I am used to dealing with conflicting demands and prioritizing my work and the work of my staff.

You can contact me as follows:

Office: xxxxx xxxxxx (extension 36)
Home: xxxxx xxxxxx (after 6.30 p.m.)
Mobile: xxxxx xxxxxx

Yours sincerely

Jill Forrester

Enc. CV

Points to pick out from this example are as follows:

- the job Jill is applying for is clearly identified at the start of her letter
- her four bullet points set out clearly and concisely the ways in which she feels she meets the criteria listed in Nifty Nimble's ad
- 'mobile' and 'prioritize' were the words Nifty Nimble used.

Notepad

When you send in an accompanying letter it is usually attached to your CV with a paper clip or a staple and, in effect, it becomes the front page. It is all the more important therefore that key 'get you to the interview' information (i.e. your strong points and your telephone contact numbers) is prominently on display.

See the Appendix (p. 138) for an example of a CV for attacking the competition.

Follow the instructions

When your CV is going to be one among dozens or even hundreds received, it is crucial that you follow to the letter any instructions given in advertisements or on websites. Do not substitute your own ideas about 'what's best', because this is how you can come unstuck.

Methods of submission

The ad will tell you how to submit your CV, i.e. by post, by fax, by e-mail, or you will have a choice. The important point is not to deviate from these instructions, for example, by faxing a CV when the ad asks you to put it in the post. It sounds harmless enough and perhaps a way of making sure you get in first but, with large numbers of applicants and employers recruiting for more than one position, there is always the risk of your CV being mislaid or put on the wrong pile. The message? You won't make a good job of engaging the competition if you're not there to do it.

Don't hang about

Occasionally an ad will give you a closing date for applications, but otherwise take it that CVs received more than five working days after an ad has appeared will stand a reduced chance of being read. What happens? Employers with vacancies are usually in a hurry to get them filled, as we saw in the example of XYZ company in Chapter 3. They wait for the flood of applications to subside (it usually takes three or four days for the flood to reduce to a trickle), then they move on to the job of sorting the wheat from the chaff and deciding who to call in for interview. Any applications received after this preliminary sort through will tend to be put to one side. Whether they will ever see the light of day again will depend on how the first trawl of interviews goes. Needless to say, their chances of success will be considerably downgraded. This is the price of procrastination.

Key point

Get a move on

Remember, the world won't wait while you're finding the time to put the finishing touches to your CV, or while other distractions are claiming your attention.

Three other 'don't's' are worth mentioning here:

- Don't use second class mail.
- Don't forget to check the weight of anything you're putting in the post. Not enough stamps means: (a) delays; and (b) your CV arriving with a postage due charge to pay (hardly a good first impression!).
- Don't outsmart yourself by delivering your application by hand. You may succeed in getting in first but you make yourself a hostage to fortune with forgetful and/or lazy receptionists and security officers.

Questions and answers

How to measure competition

Q *When I apply for a job, how do I know how much competition I am going to be up against?*

A The short answer is that you don't, but you can make an inspired guess by looking at how you sourced the job. For instance, did you see it advertised in a newspaper or journal with a wide circulation (e.g. a national)? If so, and if the job is a good job, take it as read that the competition will be intense. On the other hand, if you heard about the job via a whisper from one of your contacts in the trade, it seems safe to assume the opposite (you made it before the competition arrived).

Defining a key achievement

Q *I'm still not clear what counts as a key achievement. In my case, I cycled across Canada in aid of a charity and, in terms of what I have done in my life, I rate this very highly. More to the point, I think it says a lot about me and should encourage employers to form a positive view of what I am capable of doing. Are you suggesting I've got this wrong?*

A Certainly not. What we're saying is that in highly competitive job situations (where you're up against ferocious competition in the shape of dozens of people who are just as good as you), you need to pull out something special in the way you put together your CV. Part of the 'something special' is to have an eye-grabbing key achievements section on the first page of your CV which pinpoints you as a red hot candidate for the position. Your trip across Canada sounds great and by all means include it (possibly under your leisure time pursuits).

Summary

Where there is a lot of competition, being suitable for a job is no guarantee that you will get an interview. You also need to:

- design a CV that passes the one-quick-read test and brings out your suitability first time
- place the most compelling reasons for giving you an interview in a prominent place, for example, on the front page
- avoid delay in sending off your application.

05

CVs for mailshots

In this chapter you will learn:
- about sending unsolicited mailshots to selected employers and how to get the best result
- how to design a CV for this purpose
- what constitutes success

Sending out mailshots

At the beginning of Chapter 1, we had the example of Doug (Example B). Doug was a design engineer working in a very specialized field (bespoke machinery for the car industry). Driven by the need to find a job with better prospects, Doug was looking to make a move. He decided therefore to send a copy of his CV to ten leading machine manufacturers to see what opportunities they might have for him.

The purpose of a mailshot

Doug was hoping to strike lucky and for his CV to land on the right desk at the right time – or alternatively that it was put in the right file.

- **right desk** means the desk of whoever is responsible for hiring people like Doug
- **right time** means arriving when there is a need to recruit someone with Doug's particular blend of skills and experience
- **right file** means that the file is revisited whenever a vacancy comes up.

Notepad

Recruitment is a time-consuming and expensive option for employers. It can include:

- **Advertising** – paying for space in newspapers and journals, and having to go through the laborious process of sifting through applications and carrying out interviews.
- **Using agencies** or **recruitment consultants** – i.e. firms who hold databases of candidates. Fast, yes, but there is a price to pay for the privilege – typically a fee in the region of 15–25 per cent of starting salary.
- **Headhunting** – the slowest and most expensive of all. Most employers would only go down this route to recruit top talent or someone with very scarce or specialist skills.

Small wonder that employers often take a short cut and revisit the candidates' CVs that they hold on file.

> **Key point**
> Having your CV on the right file is a way of getting a preview of the employer's vacancies before they're advertised or put out to recruitment consultants – a case of getting in before the competition arrives!

The task an unsolicited CV has to perform

Staying with this last point, your unsolicited CV could connect with a vacancy that has already been advertised. In other words, the employer is in the process of recruiting and adds your CV to the list. However, the idea behind a mailshot is not to source jobs that are already out on the market, but to prise out two types of opportunity:

1 Where the employer is thinking about recruiting but hasn't got round to it yet.
2 Where your CV generates sufficient interest to incline an employer into thinking, 'Can we create a slot for this person?'

What is significant about both of these situations is that competition with other candidates won't be a major issue. Great? You would think so, but there is a difficulty with this. Employers receive dozens of unsolicited CVs, most of them from time-wasters, and unless something immediately connects in the mind of the reader, the tendency is to bin them. In other words, they never reach the magic file that employers pull out when they next have a need to recruit.

Designing a CV for a mailshot

On the face of it, designing a CV for a mailshot seems fraught with difficulty. There is no advertisement to look at:

• nothing to tell you what an employer views as important
• nothing to give you clues on how to prioritize your key skills and achievements.

Warning

Faced with this situation, many candidates respond by putting together a standard multi-purpose version of their CV, and sending it out to all and sundry with an equally standard covering letter. This can work for people who have highly sought-after skills but, for most of us, it's probably the best way of ensuring that our unsolicited CV ends up being fed into the shredding machine.

Research your market

Before you start ask yourself two questions:

1 Who will I be sending my CV to?
2 Why will they be interested in me?

If we go back to the example of Doug, we saw how he intended to send his CV to ten leading machine manufacturers. Why should they be interested in him? Presumably because of his experience in designing special purpose machines – consequently, this is the information that he needs to give prominence to when putting together his CV. Is there anything else that might interest them? This is where the research comes in. What does Doug know about these ten firms? For example, does he know what computer-aided design software they use? Does he know what kind of projects they work on? No? Then this is the cue for Doug to see if he can find out.

How does he do this? A good place for Doug to start is by tapping into his networks:

- Does he know anyone who has ever worked for any of these companies? If so, what can they tell him?
- Does Doug ever come into contact with people who work for these companies? For instance, is he a member of any industry groups or professional associations where he may get to meet such people?
- What about the people who supply his firm with design software? Could they pass on any interesting inside information to him?
- Presumably these ten machine manufacturers compete for business with his employers. In which case, his colleagues in sales will probably be a mine of information on how they operate.

The point is that from making a few phone calls you can extend your knowledge of the employers on your mailing list quite considerably. You can start to form a picture of what there is about you that will interest them. The watchword here is 'ask'.

Strike the chords

Remembering that employers receive large numbers of unsolicited CVs, mark yours out for special attention by positioning what is interesting about you in a prominent place. How do you do this? In the same way that you did when you designed a CV for attacking competition (see Chapter 3):

- place the interesting information in bullet-point form on the front page (in your key skills/achievements section)
- back up your application with detail in the relevant section in the body of your CV (e.g. your employment history)
- relegate (reduce to terse descriptions) any information that isn't relevant to this particular employer.

Define your ambition

This is important with a mailshot. Tell the reader in precise terms what you are looking for. Without this information, he or she won't have a clue about why you have submitted your CV.

Warning

Returning to the example of Doug, providing he puts his CV together correctly he shouldn't have too much trouble catching the eye of an employer in the same trade because someone who works for a competitor is always an intriguing prospect. Where the difficulties could arise for Doug is with time-wasting. He may find he gets invited to ten interviews with all the attendant problems of taking time off work only to discover that none of the jobs on offer are any better than the one he has. How to stop this happening? Follow the advice in Chapter 2 and make sure that your CV says enough about what you're looking for (type of job, salary, etc.) to enable readers to form an opinion about whether they have anything to interest you or not. Remember the need to be employer-friendly.

See the Appendix (p. 141) for an example of a CV for a mailshot.

Organizing a mailshot

When you send out unsolicited CVs you are never quite sure what's going to happen. At one extreme, you could hear nothing (we will deal with this situation a little later on). At the other, you could be inundated with requests to attend interviews and this could put your ability to have time off work under more strain than it can take.

Send out unsolicited CVs in small batches

Taking time off work may not be a problem for you if, for example:

- you're unemployed
- you're a student
- your employer is happy for you to take time off work, e.g. if you're in a redundancy situation and your employer is supporting you in your efforts to find another job
- you work part-time or on shifts and you have free time during the day
- your movements aren't closely supervised.

Otherwise (and because of the unpredictability of the situation), it is better to send out unsolicited CVs in small batches – say, half a dozen at a time with a space of three or four weeks between each batch.

Notepad

As we have seen putting together a CV to send out 'cold' to an employer calls for: (a) spadework in the form of research; and (b) time spent in front of the screen. For this reason, sending out CVs in small batches will be far more manageable for you.

Be selective with your mailing list

Unless your situation is desperate (e.g. you're out of work or you've just found out your name is on a redundancy list), pick and choose employers to put on your mailing list. Remember, your unsolicited CV will have far more impact where it strikes a chord. This is a case of the more targeted the effort, the better the reward. Conversely, sending CVs to employers whose names you have picked randomly out of the phone book achieves little apart from providing fodder for their shredding machines.

Send your CV to the right person

'Right' in this context means the person responsible for hiring people like you. For example, if you're an accountant, the right person will probably be the financial manager, and so on. Give the company a ring before you put anything in the post. Explain what you're seeking to do and ask for a name. Don't be fobbed off with the name of the human resources manager. Human resources managers have bigger piles of unsolicited CVs on their desks than anyone else, whereas people like financial managers won't be quite so inundated.

Put together a covering letter

Keep your covering letter to a brief explanation of:

- who you are
- what you have got to offer (your list of bullet points)
- why you're sending in an unsolicited CV (what you're looking for)
- how you can be contacted.

Warning
Don't succumb to the temptation of running off a set of standard letters with spaces left blank for writing in names, etc. No one likes to feel they're part of a mailshot. It certainly won't encourage a response.

Mark your envelope 'confidential'

This will help to ensure that your CV is seen by the right pair of eyes and not re-routed to the human resources department from some central mail reception point.

Evaluating the results

How do you measure the success of a mailshot? How do you know that your CV is doing its job?

Don't expect a reply

One of the difficulties of sending out a batch of unsolicited CVs is that often you hear nothing back – not even an acknowledgement. Whether employers should write back to everyone who sends in an unsolicited CV is a matter of opinion. Some do, some don't, and this is a fact you will have to learn to live with. The mistake, however, is to view lack of response as evidence of failure. What happens in many cases is that an unsolicited CV finds its mark (the right person), gets read with interest then, because there are no suitable vacancies at the present time, it is put on the file that will come out the next time the employer has a vacancy. The CV has done its job but, because the candidate hears nothing, he or she views the exercise as a waste of time.

Key point

When evaluating the success of unsolicited CVs, don't base your judgements on how many polite letters of acknowledgement you receive. Focus on what really matters, which is:

- connecting with opportunities that haven't yet surfaced on the job market
- making sure unadvertised opportunities never surface because you got in first.

Take stock

Quantifying the success of unsolicited CVs is notoriously difficult not only because of the lack of feedback, but also because much depends on your marketability. To illustrate, someone who is well qualified with a range of in-demand skills will attract far more interest than someone who doesn't have the same attributes. However, if you are getting no joy at all from your mailshots other than the occasional standard acknowledgement letter, it may be time to stop and take stock. Are you doing something wrong? The following checklist might help you to put your finger on the problem:

- Revisit your CV and perhaps get some second opinions. Leave your CV alone if the only flaws you pick up are minor ones.
- Are you mailing the right employers? Are you sending your unsolicited CVs to organizations who have little or no use for someone with your blend of skills, qualifications and experience?

- Are your salary expectations over the top? Go back to what we had to say on this subject in Chapter 2.
- Check your telephone contactability. Could it be that you're not there when employers are trying to get hold of you?

Questions and answers

Concerns about privacy

Q *I don't want my boss to find out that I'm looking for another job because I know she would take it personally and make life very difficult for me. For this reason I don't like the idea of sending my CV on spec to a lot of different people who may or may not be trustworthy. How do you address these concerns? I hope I've made it plain that I don't want to take any risks.*

A Sending your unsolicited CV to a named individual in an envelope marked 'Confidential' (as we suggest) will go some way towards addressing your concerns. However, unsolicited CVs are not always treated with the fullest respect when they arrive at their destination so the fears you voice have some foundation. If privacy is an issue, mailshots may not be for you. Put your effort into other methods of job seeking.

Phoning before you write

Q *Why not phone up first before sending in a CV? In this way you would find out if there are any suitable vacancies and avoid unnecessary time-wasting?*

A View cold-calling – which is what you are suggesting – and mailshots as two quite different methods of sourcing jobs. A cold-call reveals a snap shot of an organization – the opportunities they have at the point in time you make the call. Mailshots also reveal the snap shot, but at the same time they have a secondary purpose (putting you in line for any future opportunities by getting your name on the right file). You could attempt to do the same with a phone call by saying, 'Can I leave my details with you in case anything interesting comes up in the future?' The upshot is your name, address and phone number are scribbled on a piece of paper and from there on we wouldn't like to take any bets on their chances of survival. Even if the piece of paper does find its way into the magic file, everyone will have forgotten who you are the next time it sees the light of day.

Follow-up phone calls

Q *Surely the best way of finding out if an unsolicited CV has found its mark is to phone up a few days after you've sent it in and ask for an opinion. Why don't you suggest this as other books I have read make a point of recommending it?*

A Managers aren't paid to give people opinions on their unsolicited CVs, and calls of the kind you describe have the potential to be intrusive, irritating or – on a bad day – downright infuriating. Hopefully this explains why we don't recommend follow-up phone calls. Also bear in mind that:

• the average firm receives a lot of unsolicited CVs
• most unsolicited CVs are time-wasters.

Faxing your CV

Q *Why not fax your CV? Won't it stand a better chance of being read?*

A The problem we have with faxes is that employers don't always have very up-to-date or well-maintained equipment:

• your CV could end up printed off on nasty crinkly paper complete with splodges and, if you're really unlucky, a big red line down the middle to warn that the fax roll is about to run out
• the print quality itself won't be up to the standard of your original
• the fax will fade if it's stored on file for any length of time
• your CV may be assembled in the wrong order or with pages missing.

Moreover, fax machines are often situated in general offices so what you intended for your 'reader's eyes only' may be seen by anyone who happens to be around, i.e. any confidentiality is potentially prejudiced.

E-mail

Q *Surely a lot of companies today store CVs on electronic databases, so isn't it better to send them by e-mail?*

A There are a number of issues to consider with e-mail:

- The average manager is inundated with e-mails and most of them are junk. The tendency is therefore to be very selective about what's saved or printed off.
- A CV submitted by e-mail will need to be printed off if the employer's storage systems are manual. Whether they can be bothered to do this is one question. Whether they will pay as much attention to its pristine appearance as you do is the other.
- You will be sending your CV to a named manager rather than to the human resources department where these computer-based systems tend to be located.

For the above reason (and at the risk of sounding like dinosaurs) our advice is to put unsolicited CVs in the post – unless you are told to do otherwise of course.

Summary

Designing a CV to use for a mailshot is a very different task from designing a CV to apply for a job advertised in a publication or on a website. With the latter, the stimulus comes from the employer and the quality of your response is what counts. With the former, the stimulus comes from you and it falls upon you to define the outcome you are seeking – the CV you put together for a mailshot needs to address this purpose.

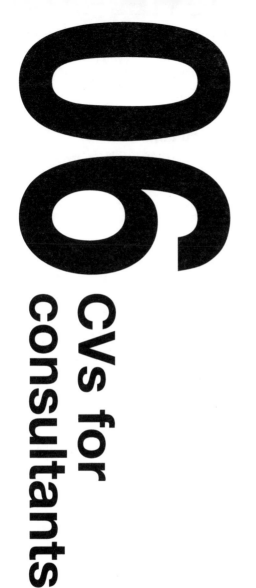

06

CVs for consultants

In this chapter you will learn:
- what drives consultants
- how to design a CV to make consultants perform for you
- about your most marketable talents and how to use them

How consultants operate

As part of your strategy for finding another job you may decide to register with a firm of recruitment consultants or an employment agency, and you will need a CV expressly for this purpose. What do you need to consider?

Bad experiences with consultants

Let's start by looking at what can go wrong. Here are two examples of people who registered with firms of consultants and felt afterwards that it was a complete waste of time.

Example 1: Adrian

'I am a quality engineer and I contacted a firm of recruitment consultants to see if they could find me a job with a higher salary. The consultant who spoke to me was very upbeat about the chances of being able to come up with something and I sent in a copy of my CV. I never heard anything from them again.'

Example 2: Lorna

'I work in sales and I am trying to get into marketing where I feel my qualifications would be put to better use. I registered with a firm of consultants who specialize in sales and marketing appointments and went to great pains to explain what I was seeking to achieve. To my annoyance they then started ringing me up every few days with jobs in sales that had just come on to their books. Every time it was a different person I spoke to; every time I had to tell them again that I didn't want a job in sales; every time they said they understood but still the calls kept coming. In the end I got fed up and told them not to ring me any more. I felt I could do better with finding a job in marketing on my own.'

What drives consultants?

So what are we looking at here? Inefficiency? People who don't listen? People who make exaggerated claims? People who style themselves as experts but who don't have a clue?

Recruitment consultants come in all shapes and sizes. Some are good and some are bad, and you need to allow for this fact (a subject we will return to later). More to the point, as you sit down to the task of designing a CV for consultants, you need to understand:

- who they are
- where they're coming from
- what they do.

No placement, no fee

The first and foremost point to understand about consultants is that they usually don't make a penny until someone starts in a job. They then charge a fee that varies from consultant to consultant, but as a rule we're talking about somewhere in the region of 15–25 per cent of starting salary, i.e. what to an outsider would seem like a large sum of money for effecting an introduction. This arrangement is known as 'no placement, no fee'.

The second point to understand about consultants is that it is customary for people who work for them to be paid on commission. This means that:

- everyone's mind is highly focused on getting placements
- candidates who are seen as easy to place get the most attention
- candidates who are seen as less easy to place can get put to one side
- in the enthusiasm to chalk up sales, the finer points in candidates' instructions often get overlooked (Lorna's experience).

Warning

There is a danger for candidates like Lorna. By repeatedly saying 'no' to consultants who ring them up, they can come across as awkward or impossible to please. In this way they can become categorized as time-wasters and the calls dry up.

Why it is important to engage with consultants

Admittedly, this may paint a bleak picture of what life is like in the recruitment business. However, the intention is not to confirm your worst fears about what goes on behind the scenes but to sharpen your mind to the task you face when you design a CV to send to a consultant.

First, let's look at where recruitment consultants fit into the job market and, more importantly, let's see what's in it for you. To do this we will take three examples of three employers who have decided to use consultants for different reasons:

Company A

'In the build up to the half-year accounts, our financial manager suddenly decided she was going to leave. Faced with the need to get someone on board quickly, we rang up three firms of recruitment consultants who specialize in financial appointments to see if they had anyone on their books who might fit the bill.'

Company B

'Our experience with advertising for staff has been poor. Typically we spend a lot of money on an advertisement then find that most of the people who apply are totally unsuitable. What we have done recently is run our vacancies through a few firms of recruitment consultants and ask them to carry out a trawl of their files. OK, it's an expensive way to hire staff but at least we don't pay unless we've taken someone on.'

Company C

'We don't have the resources or expertise to sift through hundreds of applications. What we tend to do with vacancies is give them to consultants. We know it costs but it saves us a lot of time and trouble.'

We can see from these three examples:

- How employers in a hurry are attracted to using consultants. A file search can usually be carried out within hours of a request being made. This contrasts with advertising where it could take weeks to arrive at a shortlist.
- How 'no placement, no fee' enables employers to see who's available on the market without it costing them anything.
- How consultants offer solutions to overstretched, lean-look companies, and how such companies are typical of today.

Key point

Dealing with consultants can be painful but they provide an important point of access into an area of the job market that would otherwise be closed to you. Don't, therefore, disengage from consultants. Instead, see the challenge as that of getting them to perform for you. View the design of your CV as an important part of this challenge.

Consultants' files

The more candidates consultants have on file, the greater the chances they have of:

• finding suitable people to match their clients' needs
• making money for themselves.

The sheer volume of people on file, particularly with the bigger consultancies, presents the first challenge to you. When the right job comes along, how do you ensure it's your name that is pulled out in the file search?

Notepad

Something to bear in mind is that preliminary file search is often done by computer.

Pick the right firms of consultants

To be of any use to you, firms of consultants need to meet the following three criteria:

1 They need to deal with people like you. For example, if you're a quantity surveyor, a firm of consultants who specialize in accountancy appointments will not be much good to you.
2 They must have a good client base.
3 They need to be effective – they need to be capable of matching you with the right kind of opportunities (with consultants, effectiveness should never be taken for granted).

Given these uncertainties, how do you go about picking the right firms of consultants?

- Are there any 'big names', i.e. major players in recruitment in whatever occupational group you belong to? Irrespective of how good they are, employers tend to go to the big names simply because of their size and prominence. Consequently, from your point of view you need to have your name on the files of any big name recruitment companies to enable you to profit from their market share.
- Do you have any friends or colleagues in the same profession who have had recent experience of dealing with firms of recruitment consultants? If so, see if you can pick their brains for leads.
- Scan the job ads in newspapers and journals. See which firms of consultants seem to be advertising for people like you.
- Is there anyone among your circle of contacts who is (or has been) active in the recruitment field (e.g. a human resources manager)? Such people tend to be mines of information on consultants. They have seen how they perform from the client point of view.

Warning
Registering with too many firms of consultants is a mistake because you can find yourself inundated with requests to attend interviews (more than you can handle). Three or four is a sensible maximum number. Consultants get fed up with candidates who won't go to interviews. They view them as time-wasters and switch their efforts to others who are more accommodating.

Designing a CV for consultants

What can you do to make sure that:

- Your name comes out in the file searches?
- You connect with the right opportunities?

Three assumptions

To understand the task you face when you design a CV to send in to a firm of consultants or an employment agency, it pays to proceed on the basis of three assumptions:

1 Any recruitment consultants you deal with will be heavily results-orientated. Your value in their eyes equates to whether they can place you in a job or not.

2 A recruitment consultancy or an employment agency is a busy place where new candidates are registering all the time and CVs arriving in the post or submitted on e-mail are subjected to bulk processing. What this means, once again, is that any messages you want to put across in your CV need to be capable of being assimilated in one quick and easy read. Otherwise your CV can end up stored in the wrong part of the databank, on the 'don't know' pile or fed into the shredding machines, i.e. places from which they are unlikely ever to be retrieved (you never hear anything again).

3 File search will be conducted by computer or manually by someone who may not have a complete understanding of what you do or the terminology you use.

Your marketable talents

Focusing on what makes you attractive to consultants (what gets their blood racing), you need to use your CV to highlight anything in your experience, range of skills, qualifications and so forth that makes you marketable – by which we mean marketable to their clients. Since you don't know their clients, this may seem like fishing in the dark. To help you identify areas of skill, experience and knowledge which will be good selling points, go back to our three examples of employers who use recruitment consultants (p. 74). What were these three fairly typical employers looking for and to what extent would you fit the bill? Note especially:

- Any scarce skills or unusual areas of experience. Employers who go to recruitment consultants often do so because they feel that: (a) they're looking for someone special; and (b) other methods of recruitment won't work for them. If you feel there is anything in your portfolio that marks you out as different from most people in your profession, make sure it is highlighted. For example, Shah is a management accountant but, because of his company's corporate development strategies, he has had more involvement with mergers and acquisitions than would be normal for someone with his background.

- Competence in core areas. Employers who go to recruitment consultants are often looking for a 'safe pair of hands', i.e. someone who can step in and do the job without any problems. In many cases this reflects employers who are in difficulty – with our Company A example the difficulty was caused by a key job holder deciding to leave suddenly and at a critical time. Such employers want someone to restore the calm, and so the brief to the consultants will be to come up with the names of people who are competent in the core areas of their job by virtue of their experience. Thus, experience in core areas of your job needs to be given prominence in any CV you design for consultants. It will give them something they can trot out to their clients parrot-fashion in response to these calls for help.

How can you bring core competencies and unusual aspects of your portfolio into prominence?

- list them in the key skills/achievements section on the front page of your CV
- back the information up with what you say about yourself in your employment history, educational achievements, etc.

See the Appendix (p. 144) for an example of a CV for consultants.

Make sure consultants understand you

It is important that consultants understand you because, as we saw in the case of Lorna, consultants tend to lock on to candidates' most marketable talents and then, unless directed otherwise, pepper them with everything that comes on to the books which seems to match these talents. Why is this a problem?

- Candidates' requirements may be ignored and they will gain no benefit from registering with the consultant. In Lorna's case all she heard about was jobs in sales – jobs that didn't interest her.
- Sooner or later consultants get fed up with candidates who keep saying 'no'. They detach their effort. The calls stop.

We don't know whether Lorna made it plain in her CV that she was looking for a job in marketing but, obvious though it sounds, you need to make sure that consultants understand what you're seeking to achieve by placing yourself in their hands. The 'ambitions' section in your CV seems the right place to flag up this message yet surprisingly many candidates either fail to say anything or don't make the message clear.

How to get the message over

- Use your CV to tell consultants what you want them to do for you (your ambitions section)
- reinforce the message by repeating it in any discussions you have with them
- reinforce it again in any documentation you are asked to complete, e.g. registration forms.
- don't use jargon (consultants and the people responsible for inputting information on to their databases and carrying out preliminary file searches may not understand you)
- keep the message short and simple
- be precise (say exactly what you want and don't leave anything to the imagination).

Key point

Remember what you are trying to achieve. If a job comes into the consultant's office which is right up your street, you want to be sure that you trigger the retrieval systems. The file search has got to throw out your name.

Keep consultants updated

As a footnote to this chapter, remember that if you update your CV for any reason (e.g. you gain a further qualification or you redefine your ideas about where you see your next step in life), you need to forward a copy of the new version to any consultants acting on your behalf. The penalty for failing to do this is two-fold. First, because the information on your CV is obsolete you won't be paired with the right kind of opportunities any more. Second, a copy of your old CV could get forwarded to an employer, resulting in confusion at interviews when you try to filter out information which is no longer relevant (hardly a good first impression).

Notepad
Updating CVs is covered in the final chapter of this book (Chapter 11: CV management).

Questions and answers

Can recruitment consultants be trusted?

Q *Like previous questioners, my worst nightmare is my boss getting to know that I'm looking for another job. What bothers me about putting my CV in the hands of consultants is something horrible going wrong – like my CV being sent to my boss by mistake. Can you offer any reassurances?*

A Only to say that any recruitment consultants worth their salt go to great pains to ensure that mistakes like you describe don't happen. Of course there is always scope for a slip-up in any fast-moving business where standards are not very consistent. In fairness, we have heard of very few substantiated cases of CVs finding their way into the wrong hands. Certainly don't disengage from consultants for this reason. Judge them on what counts – their performance.

Consultants for temporary work

Q *I want to do part-time temporary work next year to pay my way through college. Will I need a CV? If so, are there any points to bear in mind?*

A Most providers of temporary work (agencies) will ask you for a CV. However, when providing one you need to take into account that agencies will be looking for two qualities above all others:

1 Your willingness and ability to take on assignments as and when they ask.
2 Your competence to carry out assignments to the satisfaction of their clients.

When designing a CV for temporary work you need to:

- make it clear what hours you can and can't work (to avoid future conflict)
- say why you want to do temporary work (the reason)
- highlight key skills, qualifications and areas of experience that back up your claims to competence in whatever field of work you wish to temp in.

Summary

Designing a CV for a consultant poses a special challenge because of the need to engage with the forces that drive such people, namely:

- success in terms of placements
- the financial rewards that follow.

In this chapter we have asked you to focus on your most marketable talents because these will be the key as far as consultants are concerned. Consultants will see you as someone they can sell to their clients, someone they can make money out of, and you need to be quite explicit to strengthen these links in their minds. Being explicit in this way is the job of your CV.

At the same time, we have stressed the need to keep consultants on the track you want them to follow and not one dictated by their ambition to chalk up more sales. Again communicating aims and ambitions properly is a prime function of your CV. Nowhere is it more important than when dealing with consultants.

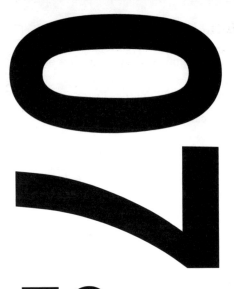

07

CVs for headhunters

In this chapter you will learn:
- how to improve your chances of being headhunted
- how to respond to an approach
- how to use your CV to dictate the terms

Getting into headhunters' nets

On the face of it, being headhunted is an event over which you have no control. The mystery phone call comes out of the blue and has no apparent connection with anything you have instigated. Yet there are steps you can take to boost your chances of being headhunted, and designing a CV for this purpose is what we will be looking at in this chapter.

See what's in it for you

First, let's consider why you should be seeking to make yourself a target for approach. There are three main reasons:

1 To open up a sector of the job market that would otherwise remain closed to you. This extends the range of your opportunities.
2 Many of the best jobs are filled by headhunting.
3 The money is flexible – it's up to employers to come up with an offer that will interest you.

Key point
Don't miss out

Headhunters operate at the very top end of the job market, and an approach from one is usually the signal that you've hit the big time. The message? Don't miss out on the opportunity that the approach provides.

The wrong way to deal with headhunters

A mistake many candidates make is to view headhunters in the same way that they view other consultants who operate in the employment field. As a result, they dig out a few names of executive search consultants (as headhunters are more properly known) and then proceed to pepper them with unsolicited CVs. What happens to these CVs? Most of them end up in the shredding machine. The lesson? Executive search consultants are not agencies or recruitment consultants, and treating them as such is not a winning strategy. Thus, any effort expended in this way is largely wasted.

Impenetrable worlds

Nevertheless, headhunters do keep files of candidates and so the question is, how do you get your name on these files and thereby onto the magical call list?

On closer inspection, headhunters' files tend to consist of two distinct categories of people:

1 Those who have been trawled in on previous assignments (people who were not placed).
2 Those who have been recommended (people kept on file because they have potential for placement in the future).

In other words, headhunters are quite choosy about who they keep on file and this choosiness has given rise to the legend that headhunters' worlds are almost impossible to penetrate. The only way in is by having the right social connections, or so the theory goes.

What drives headhunters?

Headhunters are like everyone else. They are in business to make money and they only make money by placing people with their clients. True (and unlike recruitment consultants), some of their fee is usually payable upfront but it is also true that:

• fees charged by headhunters are considerably larger than fees charged by recruitment consultants, i.e. more is at stake
• headhunters mostly get business by word of mouth recommendation, so future billings are on the line with any candidates they place.

What this boils down to is that headhunters are ultra-cautious. Yes, they need to place people in positions, but they won't want anyone on their files who they can't vouch for. The worst scenario for them is to place a candidate in a top position with a client and to find soon afterwards that the client is complaining that the candidate is useless – the headhunter can forget any repeat business!

Plan of action

So where does this leave you? Hopefully with a better understanding of:

• the task you face
• why sending an unsolicited CV to a headhunter does not tend to move you very far forward.

What must you do instead? Here is a plan of action:

- Play headhunters at their own game – use your connections to open the doors.
- Do you know anyone who has been headhunted? Think hard because it is a near certainty that someone among your circle of friends and business contacts has been on the receiving end of an approach. If so, get the name and phone number of the consultant involved.
- Ring up first, i.e. before e-mailing your CV or putting it in the post.
- Drop names. Tell the headhunter that you know so-and-so who he or she placed in a job with ABC company X years ago.
- Move on quickly to saying who you are, where you're coming from and what you are seeking to achieve in career terms. Don't embellish the facts, but do mention briefly any unusual or specialist areas of experience or skill (attributes that the headhunter may find interesting).
- Remember the aim is to get your CV onto the headhunter's files so ask if it's OK to send one in and, if so, what is the preferred method of submission, i.e. by post, fax or e-mail.
- Prick up your ears if the headhunters say that he or she can't help. It probably means that you are speaking to the wrong headhunter.
- Send the CV in quickly and while your phone call is still fresh in the headhunter's memory. Put together an accompanying letter (or lead sheet in the case of a fax). Mention your contact's name again.

Warning

Note that headhunters won't accept you at face value for the reasons we have already mentioned. They will carry out checks into your background and may ask for your assistance in doing this. What they find out about you will determine whether they view you as a good prospect or not. Consequenty, if you have blemishes on your character or your track record is poor, none of this may work.

What to bring out in your CV

Guidelines for preparing a CV for a headhunter are similar to those for preparing a CV for a recruitment consultant. Again, you need to focus on your most marketable talents and to highlight any unusual or specialist areas of experience or skill. Headhunting assignments frequently involve finding people who are out of the ordinary, people who:

• are not in abundant supply
• other methods of recruitment won't reach.

Receiving headhunters' approaches

Imagine you're sitting at home one evening, relaxing and watching TV, when the phone rings and someone you've never heard of before is on the other end of the line asking you if you would be interested in a top position with one of their clients. How do you respond?

Don't shut doors

Approaches often arrive when you least expect them. When the call comes, you may not be actively looking for another job. Indeed, you may be perfectly happy with the job you have. So, when someone comes on the phone and asks you if you would be interested in making a move, the natural inclination is to say 'no'. Why is this a mistake?

• You could be turning your back on the opportunity of a lifetime. As we know, opportunity rarely knocks twice.
• From your remarks, the headhunter could assume that you're not interested period. You have given a signal to strike you off the call list. This is not what you want.

Key point
Stay engaged

Keep the approaches coming. Do this by being positive with headhunters and engaging with them.

Move the approach forward

With any approach, your aim at the initial stages should be to keep it moving forward. Therefore, when a headhunter asks you if you are in the market for making a move, always reply along the lines that whilst you are perfectly happy with what you're doing now (true or not) you would always be interested to hear about any opportunity to move your career forward. This then puts the ball in the headhunter's court. Why did he or she ring you? More specifically:

- What's the job?
- Why you?

As we shall see shortly, the answers to these two questions will have a bearing upon the crafting of your CV.

What's the job?

Here you may run into two obstacles:

1 The headhunter may not wish to divulge too much information, and the client's identity probably won't be disclosed to you until later in the selection process.
2 The person you speak to (the mystery voice) may be a researcher hired by the headhunter, i.e. he or she may not be in direct contact with the client.

This is often a case for doing the best you can, i.e. pump for as much information as possible. Your pretext for doing this is to establish:

- whether the position in question is a move in the right direction for you
- whether the position would interest you or not.

The aim is to find out enough about the position to enable you to form a view about what qualities are being sought in candidates.

Why you?

Why have you been approached? Did someone recommend you? If so, for what reason? The answer to these questions will hopefully tell you what the headhunter sees as your strong points for the position. Is it your experience? Or do you have contacts that the headhunter's client would find useful? Alternatively, do you have specialist knowledge or skills that the client is anxious to acquire?

Key point
Pick headhunters' brains

See the headhunter as someone who is on your side. As we have mentioned previously, there are rich pickings to be had from successful headhunting assignments and, given your suitability, the headhunter has a vested interest in you getting the job.

A CV for when you are headhunted

Once the preliminaries are out of the way and you have indicated your interest in anything that moves your career forward, the headhunter will probably ask you to send in a copy of your CV.

Warning
In the excitement to get something in the post, candidates often succumb to the temptation to send a standard off-the-peg CV, e.g. the one they used when they last applied for a job. Don't. Being headhunted offers a unique opportunity to make big steps forward in your career and, whilst you should never dilly-dally, it's worth devoting some time and effort to producing a CV that will have more chance of a successful outcome (successful for you, that is).

What to say about yourself

Armed with some information about the position for which you've been headhunted and why you've been singled out as a target, you now know what you need to highlight when it comes to the design of your CV. Here, the drill is the same as that for highlighting key areas of skill and experience when you apply for jobs you have seen advertised:

- list your strong points on the front page of your CV under the heading of your key skills and achievements
- back up the information about your strong points by developing the detail in your job history, education, training, etc.

Notepad

An important difference with CVs that you send to headhunters is that they won't get the one-quick-read treatment. They will be scrutinized carefully – headhunters focus their attention on a select and relatively small number of people. Moreover, there are not the same constraints on the length of a CV and, whilst the rules on conciseness and relevance still apply, you should feel no inhibition about expanding strong areas of your application simply for reasons of space.

Set out your stall

Being headhunted gives you the chance to get a good deal for yourself. The fact that someone wants you badly enough to go to the expense and trouble of headhunting you indicates that you are in a strong bargaining position and you shouldn't hesitate to take advantage.

How do you do this? The first step is to set out your stall and to use your CV for this purpose. You need to state clearly and unequivocally what it will take to tempt you out of your tree, for example, pay, perks, contractual terms.

Key point

Get the best deal you can

Employers normally enter into an approach with very flexible ideas about the kind of package it will take to attract the right calibre of candidate, and there is usually plenty of scope for negotiation. In setting out your stall, therefore, don't fall into the trap of asking for too little. Remember that:

* in any negotiation it's easier to come down than it is to talk your way back up
* by asking for too little you could give the impression that you are lacking in personal ambition, and this could be seen as a bad point in a candidate for a top job
* your CV will be read by a headhunter who is used to talking salaries in truly astronomical figures without blinking an eyelid. 'Being too greedy' or 'going over the top' has no meaning to them.

See the Appendix (p. 147) for an example of a CV for a headhunter.

Questions and answers

No connections

Q *Perhaps I live in a narrow world but I don't know anyone who's been headhunted. I take the point about unsolicited CVs and the tendency to bin them, but I don't see that I have any alternative other than putting one in the post and hoping for the best. What do you say?*

A Headhunting is so prevalent – especially with senior appointments – that we wonder how much effort you've put into tapping your networks. Given, however, that you can't come up with the name of a friend or colleague who has been headhunted then the advice to 'phone first' (i.e. before putting a CV in the post) still holds good. Be prepared to have to sell yourself a little harder, that's all.

Asking for too much and putting headhunters off

Q *Surely if I put a salary expectation in my CV which is way over the top, it will only serve to frighten headhunters off. What's the answer to this?*

A If you've done your research properly, you will know that there is a range of salaries available to people with your particular blend of experience, qualifications and skills. With an approach, we're suggesting that you start the negotiation at the top end of the range, i.e. the top end figure is the one that needs to go in your CV. As to frightening headhunters off, we feel this is unlikely. They will know how far their client will stretch to get the right person on board, and if your ideas are way out of line the headhunter will probably tell you. You will then be left with the option of:

- **either** adjusting your expectations down a notch or two
- **or** saying you're not interested.

Where the approach comes directly from an employer

Q *I was headhunted recently, except in my case the approach was from a rival business rather than an executive search consultant. I have been asked to send in a CV but, realizing the situation is different, is there anything I need to consider?*

A In fact, most headhunting is carried out directly by employers, and your experience of a poaching excursion by a competitor is fairly typical. Is there anything you need to consider? Again, try and find out as much about the job as you can and why you've been singled out for the approach because this will tell you what you need to highlight when it comes to designing your CV. Don't be afraid to name your price, and don't sell yourself cheap (the competitor clearly needs you). One difficulty with a direct approach is that you don't have the headhunter acting as an intermediary. This means that it's down to you to keep the momentum going.

Headhunters who offer to design your CV

Q *A firm of headhunters who contacted me recently said they would produce a CV for me and then quoted a price which seemed very expensive. Am I right to be wary?*

A Yes you are. Bona fide executive search consultants make their money by providing a service to their clients, not by charging candidates for writing their CVs. Anyone who makes a proposal like this should be viewed with great suspicion. Distance yourself from them immediately.

Summary

In this chapter we have been looking at designing CVs for two different purposes:

1 A CV for headhunters' files – here the challenge is to overcome the cautiousness of headhunters when it comes to dealing with people they don't know.
2 A CV to use when you are targeted for an approach.

We have tried to impress upon you that there are rich rewards to be had from being headhunted. Going that extra mile with the design of your CV is time and effort well invested.

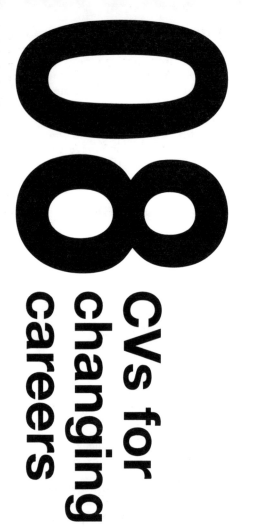

08

CVs for changing careers

In this chapter you will learn:
- about the challenge of making a move into a completely new field
- how to design a CV to address this challenge
- how to identify and use your transferable talents
- how to overcome employers' concerns

Where are you coming from?

Somewhere along your path in life, you may decide to make a complete change of career. How do you design a CV to help you break into:

- a completely fresh field?
- a field in which you have little or no experience?

Let's begin by making a distinction. Career changes can be divided into two types:

1 **Visionary career changes:** those that are driven by a dream or ambition.
2 **Forced career changes:** those that you have to make (the no choice situations).

Here are two examples:

Example A: Visionary

Caroline has worked as an administrator in a hospital for the last seven years – a job she has started to find boring. Caroline feels her best attribute is people. She deals with people in her job, and this is the part she enjoys most. She wants to become a human resources manager and, with this ambition in mind, she has been doing a part-time evening course at her local college of adult education. When she finishes the course, she plans to start applying for jobs in human resources management, and she has already given some thought to how she will market herself.

Example B: Forced

Dean works as a site manager for a construction company. Dean's job involves climbing ladders and scaffolds but, following an operation, his doctor advised him against working at heights or anywhere where he could be at risk from falls. Dean realizes this means an end to his career in construction site management. He will have to look for something different. He is currently off work sick, but he knows his absence is causing problems for his employer and soon they will be asking him questions.

Which type do you fit into?

The challenges facing Caroline and Dean are clearly very different, and this is why it's important at the outset of any career change to decide which of these two types you fit into. Are you, like Caroline, being driven by a vision? Or has your career change been forced on you by an alteration of circumstances similar to Dean's case?

Fixed and flexible ideas

From the point of view of designing a CV, the main difference to focus on between a visionary and a forced career change is the extent to which your ideas are fixed or flexible:

- with Caroline we saw that she had entertained no other ideas apart from breaking into a career in human resources management
- with Dean, on the other hand, we saw how his ideas were flexible – in fact it is probably true to say that someone in his position would be happy to consider anything within reason.

Timescale

Another important difference between visionary career changes and those that are forced upon you is the timescale you are working to. In the case of Caroline, she is in no particular hurry to see her ambitions realized, whereas with Dean, the length of time he can be off work with a sick note is limited by the constraints of his employer's business. The clock is ticking, and this is something he needs to consider.

Notepad

Forced career changes can arise from a number of situations, for example:

- if your line of work is associated with a particular industry or sphere of activity, and that industry or sphere of activity closes down in the area where you live
- if your personal circumstances change, for example, you become responsible for the care of dependants whereas previously you had a job which required you to be mobile and flexible.

Transferable talents

Changing careers is about taking your bundle of skills, qualifications, experience and personal attributes and applying them to something else (something different). Not all of your talents are transferable, however. For example, many of the techniques and know-how that Caroline has acquired in her time at the hospital won't have any relevance to a career in human resources management. On the other hand, some of her talents are transferable, for instance, her people skills.

> **Key point**
> **Focus on the facilitators**
>
> Focus on your transferable talents. They are the facilitators as far as your change of career is concerned. Transferable talents need to be highlighted in your CV.

The task ahead of you

At the outset of any change of career, you won't know:

- how difficult it will be
- how long it will take.

There is a problem for people like Dean, people who have had their career changes forced upon them. They are constantly racing against the clock and sometimes it beats them. The career change they hoped for didn't come off in the time they had available. They end up out of work or doing fill-in jobs, and at the same time they usually have financial pressures to contend with.

Multiple-targeting

However, people in forced career change situations are usually prepared to consider anything. So, in the case of someone like Dean, he could investigate a number of ideas – not just one. To illustrate, he could apply his transferable management skills outside the construction industry, i.e. to situations where there are no risks posed by falls. Also, he probably has a good knowledge of safety law and this knowledge could be transferred into, say, working as a trainer or selling personal protective equipment. The list goes on, but the point is that Dean should be pursuing all of these options simultaneously because:

- it will increase his chances
- it will allow for the fact that some changes of career may take longer than the time he has available (something he won't know in advance).

> **Key point**
> Therefore, Dean needs to make sure that the design of his CV takes into account this multiple-targeting. He needs different versions of his CV depending on which new career he is targeting. He should identify which of his transferable talents are applicable to each career and, conversely, which are not.

Addressing employers' concerns

Don't expect employers to fall over backwards to come up with the openings which will enable your change of career. Expect instead a certain amount of reticence. They have met people like you before and the experience has not always been very gratifying. They will want to know:

- Whether you are serious.
- If you have thought through the money implications of changing career (going back to being a beginner usually entails taking a drop in earnings).
- What you have done to prepare for your new career. For example, have you been on any courses?

Employers' experiences

Employers have had their fingers burned, notably with:

- people who lack commitment; people who don't stay very long; people who go back to the jobs they did previously
- people who discover they can't manage on reduced pay; people who start grumbling and/or asking for rises
- people who do nothing about their training; people who expect their employers to provide the facilities and foot the bills.

Key point
Overcome the obstacles

If you are seeking to move into a new career by shopping around on the job market for suitable opportunities, you will have to face up to competition from people who are experienced. In a world where employers play safe when it comes to new faces, it will be up to you to demonstrate:

- that you are serious; that you have researched your ideas properly and they are not something that popped into your head randomly
- that you have planned your finances to take into account the need to live on a reduced salary
- that you have already taken some steps to realize your career change ambitions.

Needless to say, your CV will play an important part in getting these messages across. You will only overcome the obstacles in employers' minds by addressing them and engaging with them – not by leaving employers to form their own opinions.

Designing a CV to facilitate a change of career

The challenges of designing a CV for the purpose of effecting a change of career can be summarized as follows:

- you need to make it clear that you are looking to change careers otherwise someone reading your CV could think that you have made a mistake and applied for the wrong job
- you need to say why you have made the decision to change careers – explain your reasons and show that you're serious
- you need to say why you feel you are suitable for the career you've chosen, and to identify any transferable areas of skill, experience, job know-how etc.
- you need to address your salary expectations and make it clear to employers that you accept that in the short term your earnings may have to fall.

Warning

Rather like changing jobs, the reasons for wishing to change career need to come across in a positive light. In particular, avoid projecting yourself unintentionally as a misfit or as someone who is perpetually discontented. Focus at all times on the benefits you perceive will result from making the move into your new career. Don't dwell on the negative by listing the bad points about the career you're in now.

Determine what's relevant

Most of the information that normally goes into a CV will be irrelevant to someone who is considering you for a completely different career, and it pays to give this some thought when putting together your CV. The detail of what you did in previous jobs may be interesting to a point, but given too much exposure it could act as a turn-off. Because it lacks relevance it will not provide an incentive to read on.

Don't send out conflicting messages

Similarly, going into raptures about the work you're doing now or the work you've done in the past seems at odds with seeking to change careers. At worst, conflicting messages such as these can come across as a lack of commitment. In this way you can damage your application.

Personal aims and ambitions

The biggest challenge is getting across in your CV the message:

- that you are seeking to change careers
- why you are changing careers
- that you're serious about changing careers.

What do you need to say? Here is an example:

Aims

I am looking to move into design, commissioning and installation of mechanical handling equipment. My reasons are as follows:

- I have worked on the maintenance of mechanical handling equipment in a fully automated assembly plant for the last nine years

- I have served a full mechanical engineering apprenticeship
- I recently did a mechanical engineering degree in my own time and passed with first class honours
- I am seeking to use my experience and qualifications to enter a more challenging field.

The points to pick out from this example are:

- it's clear and concise – no one reading it is left in any doubt that this is someone seeking to move out of a hands-on job into a professional career
- it's positive – the candidate doesn't air any gripes about still working on the tools
- it identifies the candidate's transferable talents
- the fact that the candidate has done a degree in his or her own time shows commitment.

Salary

Many candidates bent on a change of career slip up by including their present earnings in their CV and leaving it at that. The signal to anyone reading the CV is that this is the level of earnings which the candidate is expecting to better or at least maintain. Since the candidate is applying for a job as a beginner, this will flag up as a mismatch and the probable outcome is that the candidate's CV will be put on the 'No thank you' pile. Certainly don't expect an employer bombarded with applications from eminently suitable candidates to take the time and trouble to ring you up to clarify matters. You are the outsider as far as this particular contest is concerned. The clarification is down to you.

Again, what do you need to say? Here is what our maintenance fitter with the first class honours degree did to overcome the problem of communicating pay expectations:

Salary

I am currently earning XX,XXX per annum of which XXX.XX is made up of shift payments. By seeking to move into a career where I will enjoy better prospects, I recognize that I may have to accept lower earnings at first. Fortunately, my partner is in well-paid employment and in this way we will be able to make up any shortfall.

Points to pick out are as follows:

- Assuming that the job of design, commissioning and installation engineer would mean working normal office times, identifying that an element of the current salary package consists of payments for unsociable hours helps any prospective employer to compare the two jobs on a like-for-like basis. Expressed in this way, the reduction in earnings is not such a big one and this may help to ease some employers' concerns.
- The reference to the partner's well-paid job demonstrates that the candidate has thought through the financial implications of changing careers and made plans accordingly. In this way it addresses another of the concerns that employers have.

Key point

Remember that employers don't have to take a chance on you. They can offer the job to someone who has a proven track record. It is your job to be proactive and pre-empt employers' concerns. Don't kid yourself that the concerns aren't there or, worse still, expect employers to address the issues. In most cases they won't bother, and really why should they?

Employment history

Going back to the relevance of the information in your CV, don't hesitate to prune out any excess detail in your job history.

Warning

Changing careers is not easy and typically you run into the brick wall of employers turning you down because of your lack of experience. Here there may be a temptation to tinker with your CV. If experience is the passport to the jobs, why not invent a little?

Making false claims about previous experience is a dangerous game. Not only do you run the risk of being found out but, more worrying in many ways, what if your little ruse succeeds? You get the job on the basis of experience that you haven't had, and this means:

- the expectation placed on you to perform will be higher than your true capability

- the normal allowances given to beginners will not be extended to you.

Finding yourself out on your ear after six months won't be a very good start to your new career. So, even though you may be finding it difficult to get interviews, always be honest with employers. If they decide to give you a chance, let it be on the basis of your limited or non-existent experience. Let them be the ones to decide whether they can live with a learner or not.

Notepad
We have written another book in the Teach Yourself series which deals with the subject of changing careers: *Teach Yourself Making Successful Career Changes*.

See the Appendix (p. 150) for an example of a CV for changing careers.

Questions and answers

Asking recruitment consultants to find the openings

Q *With a change of careers, do you feel it's a good idea to register with an agency or a firm of recruitment consultants? Will they be able to help me? If so, what special pointers are there on what needs to go in my CV?*

A The answer to the first part of your question is yes, recruitment consultants can help you to access the invisible market by using their contacts – the part of the market where there is less competition and where employers won't be viewing you alongside hundreds of other candidates, all with more experience. With regards to the design of your CV, you need to make it abundantly clear to any recruitment consultants you choose that you are seeking to make a change of career. This is to stop them hounding you with vacancies in the field in which you currently work (the experiences of Lorna in Chapter 6 are worth bearing in mind). Remember too that agencies and consultants are results-orientated and they will naturally gravitate towards pursuing openings in the line of work where you would be easiest to place, i.e. the line of work in which you have experience.

Will employers take advantage of me?

Q *Putting in my CV that I am prepared to take a drop in earnings is surely an invitation to employers to take advantage of me. What do you say to this?*

A The bigger danger is that employers may assume from reading your CV that you're expecting the same money that you're earning now to do a beginner's job. The result will be that you get no interviews. As for starting salaries, it is more important at this point to break into your new career. With experience, you will be able to negotiate a better salary – either with your employer or by shopping around on the job market. Without experience, you will get nowhere.

No interviews – is my CV at fault?

Q *I am a machine tool engineer and for the last 12 months I have been trying to get into sales because: (a) my present job brings me into contact with customers and (b) I feel I am good at dealing with people. I have applied for over 20 jobs and up to now I have not succeeded in getting one single interview. I am starting to think that my CV could be the reason for my lack of success. Do you have any advice on what I should do?*

A Twenty job applications and no interviews would seem like a poor performance and, yes, in the face of such evidence it would be normal to look at your CV and see if there are any ways in which you could improve it. However, job applications aimed at breaking into a completely new field aren't normal, and you need to use a different measure of success to the one you use for job applications in a field in which you have experience. You are successful if you keep going against what can sometimes seem like almost insurmountable odds. You fail if you give up. Any other advice? It seems like you're focusing all of your attention on the visible or advertised job market where competition from people with experience is going to be at its greatest. With career changes you may have more joy from tapping into the invisible market, for example:

- send your CV to selected employers together with a suitably worded accompanying letter
- spread the word around among your contacts (networking).

With the second of these bullet points, your knowledge of machine tools would seem to be the facilitator – the transferable talent. So how about your contacts in the machine tool industry? Could they put a word in the right ear for you and possibly pull a few strings? Our research shows that more people get their breaks by networking than in any other way, and any effort expended in this direction is well worth it.

Summary

Changing careers is intrinsically difficult because it means moving out of a field in which you have experience into one where you will be viewed as an absolute beginner. Clearly 'something special' is called for, and this is how you should view the task of putting together a CV for this purpose.

In this chapter we have looked at the need:

- to communicate your ambitions clearly and concisely
- to explain yourself, and to convince employers that you're not indulging in a flight of fancy or have taken leave of your senses
- to broach the subject of salary and let employers see that: (a) you're not living in cloud cuckoo land; and (b) you've given some thought to living on reduced earnings.

09

CVs for business

In this chapter you will learn:
- about CVs for people who work for themselves
- about CVs to source work
- about CVs to present to financial institutions
- the different test of relevance

People who work for themselves

What about people who work for themselves? You may think that someone who is self-employed and operating independently or as a small business has no requirement for a CV. However, let's consider two quite different examples:

Example 1: Alice

Alice is a freelance IT trainer who is seeking to expand her client base by approaching firms who have moved onto a new business park in the town where she lives. In the case of one of these firms, the general manager has expressed an interest in the service she provides but, before committing himself further, he has requested to see a copy of her CV.

Example 2: Rick and Deborah

Rick and his partner Deborah operate a sandwich-making and delivery service to offices in the local area. Rick and Deborah have seen their business triple in the last two years, and now need to take out a lease on larger premises as well as purchase new equipment, including a second van. Originally they approached their bank for the funds and overdraft facilities they felt they needed but, to their dismay, they found their bank unreceptive to the case they put forward. As a result, they approached another bank and found an entirely different and more supportive attitude. However, as part of the bank's process of vetting new business accounts, it has asked both Rick and Deborah to provide a CV.

Warning

Because people who work for themselves are not in the market for jobs, they may not see any reason to have a CV. As a consequence, if they find themselves in situations like those of Alice, Rick and Deborah, they are faced with starting from scratch. The message? Just because you are outside the world of normal employment, don't assume you will never need a CV. People who you will have to deal with sometimes need to have more information on who you are, what you've done and your qualifications. Be ready for this when it happens.

The test of competence

Before engaging Alice to provide IT training to his staff, the general manager of the new company on the business park needed to see that she was competent to do the job. He needed to see that:

- she was qualified to teach IT
- her knowledge of software packages included those used by his company
- she had a proven track record as a service provider (that she had a client list)
- she could deliver, i.e. she was going to be there when the need for training arose.

This is why he asked to see a copy of her CV.

The test of suitability

Rick and Deborah approached a bank who'd had no previous dealings with them. Therefore, before granting overdraft and loan facilities to their business the bank needed to see that:

- the business was viable
- they would not default on repayments
- their expansion plans were well-founded
- they had the commitment and character to carry the plans through.

The bank would doubtless be asking Rick and Deborah to provide all kinds of financial information to back up their case. Their CVs would form part of the supporting evidence – a further testimony to who they are and what makes them suitable people to advance money to and take on trust.

Key point
It is evident in both of these scenarios that the CVs which Alice, Rick and Deborah have been asked to produce will be required to perform very different tasks to those that CVs are normally expected to perform.

Further considerations

To satisfy yourself that someone like Alice is going to be a good IT training provider – enough to give her a chance – you would pose a different set of questions to those you would pose if you were looking at Alice as a candidate for a job. True, you can chop and change service providers in a way that would be difficult with ordinary employees. Yet engaging someone to come in and do a job like training staff implies that you have the confidence in them to perform that function. If it all goes wrong, and the service provider proves to be useless, there is egg on the faces of the people who hired them.

Warning

People in senior management positions have all had their fingers burned at one time or another by service providers who do not live up to their promises. Since the credibility of the organization is often at stake, the same managers will tend to be choosy about who they take on trust (who they do business with).

Staying with the example of Alice, it is interesting to reflect on the concerns of people like the general manager of Alice's prospective new client – concerns such as how consistent and reliable she is going to be. For example, let's say that Alice has only been in business as an IT trainer for six months. One of the concerns might then be about her commitment to being a service provider. Is she only in it for the short term? Is she doing it while she's looking for another job? If so, what happens to the service when she finds something?

Part of the problem here, of course, is that the general manager of the new firm on the business park doesn't know anything about Alice's background. She's approached him out of the blue and he needs reassurances which go beyond reassurances about her competence. Where does he get such reassurances? The answer is from her CV.

Key point
Address all the concerns

A CV used by a self-employed person to source work needs to address *all* the potential concerns. In the case of Alice, if she hasn't been in business very long her CV may need to explain to her prospective clients:

- why she decided to set up in business as a service provider
- how she's getting on
- her long-term commitment to the role.

Admittedly, a lot of this information could be imparted in face-to-face discussions, but don't neglect to back up what you say by including it in your CV. Rather like a job interview, view the face-to-face meeting as an extension of the messages that are in your CV.

Now let's turn to Rick and Deborah. What concerns might the bank have about them, and how could these concerns be addressed by what they put in their respective CVs?

When a business grows in the way that Rick and Deborah's sandwich service has grown, the roles of the people running the business inevitably change. Whereas in the early days, Rick and Deborah were probably hands on, preparing the sandwiches and doing the deliveries themselves, their roles in the enlarged organization will become more administrative and managerial. Sooner or later they will probably take on staff to do the hands on tasks, and the managerial part of their job will grow. More to the point, the future success of their venture will depend on how good they are as managers, and this will form part of any critical appraisal of their prospects by an institution such as a bank.

What has this got to do with Rick and Deborah's CVs? Simply that if either of them has had any previous managerial experience (e.g. responsibility for the work of others) this is something that needs to be brought out and given prominence in their CVs.

Key point
Second-guessing

As a self-employed person, second-guessing what recipients of your CV are looking for is not dissimilar to the second-guessing that employed people do when they're putting together a CV to apply for a job. In one case, the second-guessing is about what employers have got at the back of their minds. In the other, the guesswork is applied to people who have an entirely different set of criteria for appraising you. The full extent of the criteria is what you need to understand.

Notepad

With partnerships such as Rick and Deborah, one of the biggest risks is that, for some reason, the partnership doesn't survive. What happens, for example, if they fall out or if one of them decides to set up in competition? Concerns such as these inevitably pass through the minds of people whose job it is to vet applications for loans and overdrafts. They need reassurances in the same way that Alice's potential client needed reassurances. In the case of Rick and Deborah, the reassurance of their staying power as a partnership might be provided by suitable evidence in their CVs. For instance, it would help to say how the two of them got together and why they decided to go into business. Many partners meet when working for the same organization, and this would be viewed as a plus point by people looking to form an assessment of their suitability to run a business as a team. The evidence of a long-standing professional relationship pre-dating the setting up of the business would help overcome any doubts about their stability as a partnership.

CVs to source work

This is where we focus upon Alice. In precise terms, what does she need to put into her CV that will help convince the general manager of her prospective new client that she will be a good person to do business with? Conversely, what's irrelevant to him (what does she need to leave out)?

Key achievements

In writing up this section of her CV, Alice needs to be careful that the key achievements she lists are relevant to her role as a training service provider. For example, if she's built up her client base from zero to 50 companies in her first three months of trading, that would be a relevant key achievement. It would also show not only that she's competent at her job, but also her commitment to making her business a success (and staying in it long term). On the other hand, the fact that she was made PA of the Year in a job she held previously won't figure too highly in a prospective client's reckoning. In fact, it may convey the impression that she is secretly hankering to be a PA again, i.e. she is only in IT training short term and as a stopgap.

Personal profile/ambitions

In this section, say why you're in business on your own account (the reason). Explain that your ambition is to go on working for yourself. Emphasize that you get your kicks out of providing your clients with a good service. Perhaps say too that you enjoy the diversity of doing work for a number of different organizations. Convey the impression that:

- you like what you do
- you went into it for good positive reasons, i.e. *not* that you couldn't find anything else to do after you were made redundant from your last job
- you don't want to do anything else.

Salary

Take this section out. You charge a price for your work and you will give details of your price and terms of business in any quotations that you submit, i.e. separately. Note that by leaving a section on salary in a CV which is intended to source freelance work, you can again create the impression that your real ambition is to get back into a mainstream job.

Qualifications, education and training

Here, you need to apply the test of relevance once more. Qualifications and courses of training that are relevant are those that have a bearing on your ability to provide the service you are offering. For example, Alice's qualifications as an IT teacher need to be given prominence, whereas qualifications she gained in some other field (and as part of her previous job role) need to be relegated or, in some cases, left out altogether.

Employment history

Details of previous jobs and what you did in those jobs are only relevant insofar as they reflect your competence to provide the service you are offering. Therefore, try as far as possible to present an overview of your past employment history. Avoid long lists of achievements and high spots because, apart from being irrelevant, it can again give the impression that you're hankering to get back into a job, i.e. your motives and commitment are unsound.

Reasons for leaving your last job

Pause here for a moment. What drives you is a major issue for anyone viewing you as a potential service provider. It won't be good if anything suggests that you're working independently because you didn't have any other option. Yes, it would be nice to say that you left your last job because you decided to set up on your own. It would demonstrate a lot of confidence and commitment (sufficient to give up a job with a regular income, take the plunge and go it alone). However, what if that wasn't the case? For instance, what if you were made redundant, and going independent was something you turned to because nothing else was available? Here the suggestion is to dress up the facts a little. OK, so redundancy was the reason your last job folded, but couldn't you say that you'd been considering branching off on your own anyway? The redundancy and the cash that went with it simply presented you with the wherewithal.

Anything else?

Look through the skeleton version of your CV and see if there's anything else that might cause concern to someone viewing you as a service provider. An example we had recently was a self-employed management consultant who was a wheelchair user.

He travelled to his clients by a combination of taxis, and getting friends and members of his family to give him lifts. This had no effect on his work but, without some explanation in his CV, he could have come across as someone with mobility and travelling difficulties. Again, the message is to spot the potential area of concern and take steps to pre-empt it.

CVs to present to financial institutions

People in business can be asked to provide CVs to support applications for loans, overdrafts or avail themselves of other financial services, as we saw with Rick and Deborah at the beginning of this chapter. Whether you will ever be called upon to do the same depends to some extent on the luck of the draw and on how often you need injections of cash.

Notepad
There is a question at the end of this chapter which goes into more detail about the chances of you being asked to provide a CV. See 'Why do I need a CV?'

To recap, the CVs that Rick and Deborah submitted in support of their loan and overdraft application needed to transmit messages that would:

• make the bank feel comfortable about granting them the facilities they wanted
• demonstrate their ability to run an enlarged organization and manage extra people, money and other resources effectively and prudently
• show their relationship with one another as: (a) stable; and (b) professional.

Key achievements

Here the focus needs to be on Rick and Deborah's achievements while working together as a team. That they have tripled their turnover in the last two years is an obvious example of a key achievement, but there will be others and, to pick the right ones to highlight, Rick and Deborah need to focus on the fact that financial achievements are likely to have most impact on institutions such as banks. Profit growth would be a good example of an achievement – as would cost control and/or the business's record with repaying previous loans. Incidentally, there is no harm at all in Rick and Deborah replicating their key achievements (putting down exactly the same information in their respective CVs). If anything, this gives the impression of two people firmly bonded and professionally committed as a team. It adds credence to their durability as a partnership and, as we saw earlier in the chapter, this will act as a comforter to an institution such as a bank.

Personal profile/ambitions

Once again this section needs to come across as a team act, with the ambition expressed in terms of the ambition of the business rather than of two separate people (lots of 'we' and 'us' instead of 'I' and 'me'). In this context, the bank would be pleased to see two people with exactly the same agenda. It speaks well for the future of the partnership and its ability to keep up the repayments on a loan.

Salary

Clearly this is irrelevant so strike it out.

Employment history

As in the case of Alice and for reasons of relevance, it will pay to say little about previous jobs (jobs held prior to the establishment of the partnership). Again, a brief overview will suffice except where previous job history:

- relates to the operational aspects of a sandwich-making and delivery service
- provides evidence of administrative and managerial experience (the point we touched upon earlier).

It would be interesting and relevant to insert some insight into the origins of the partnership in this section. For example, did Rick and Deborah once work together for the same company? If so, say so and explain in what capacities. Two colleagues getting together and hatching a plan to start a business could have particular appeal to a bank because it demonstrates the ability to put ideas into action and bring them to fruition.

Qualifications, education and training

Qualifications to highlight are those that go with the operation of a successful sandwich-making business. Other than general educational qualifications to show that Rick and Deborah are capable of dealing with the basics, this includes qualifications and training in such subjects as food hygiene and safety. Also of relevance, for the reasons we've discussed, is any evidence of qualifications and training in commercial and/or managerial disciplines and skills.

Anything else?

It is important to identify anything in your CV that could raise a question mark in the mind of the person reading it. The person in this case is someone who will be sizing up whether you are a good risk from a financial institution's point of view. Hence, anything in your CV that comes into conflict with what might be seen as a 'good risk' needs to be suitably qualified.

Notepad

If you've been in business before and if for any reason the business has ceased trading, you need to be quite explicit in any case you put to a financial institution about:

- the circumstances
- how any outstanding debts including loans were paid off.

This is a classic case of financial institutions assuming the worst unless they're told differently.

See the Appendix (p. 153) for an example of a CV for business.

Questions and answers

Why do I need a CV?

Q *I've been in business for over 20 years and in that time no one has ever asked me for a CV. Are you suggesting I prepare one 'just in case'? If so, isn't this taking matters a little too far?*

A As a self-employed person, your need for a CV will have a lot to do with the nature of your business and to what extent it is static or expanding. For example, if you are a self-employed electrician doing commercial and domestic wiring installations and you get most of your work through a network of local building contractors who've known you for years then, no, there's not going to be much call for you to produce a CV. On the other hand if, like Alice, you're one of the growing band of professionals who operate independently and you are constantly striving to expand your client base, it could be a very different story.

Portfolio working

Q *Like Alice in your example, I make a living as a self-employed trainer except in my case I offer training in stress management skills. A little over three months ago my biggest client (accounting for approximately 60 per cent of my turnover) went into liquidation and I was left with the job of having to find enough new business to plug the hole and keep the wolf from the door. Sadly my fortunes were mixed and, whilst I did pick up a few new accounts, any new business did not go far enough to make up the huge shortfall in my earnings. Luckily for me, however, I hold a heavy-goods vehicle driving licence which dates from my time in the armed forces. I appreciate it sounds strange, but I think I can make enough money to keep my finances afloat by temping as a driver for two days a week – at least until such a time when I have some more names on my client list. However, I realize that to get temping work I will need to be on the books of an agency and that means they will want to see a copy of my CV. Given these circumstances, what do I put in my CV? Do I need to conceal from the agency that I'm using them as a stop gap? If so, how do I do it?*

A We will answer your question in two parts. First, don't see your situation as anything out of the ordinary. People who work for themselves frequently have to make up short-term shortfalls, and what easier way to do it than to pick up the odd bit of temping work? In your case, you have the added advantage of a skill which is in short supply, and getting work at a favourable rate of pay should not present a problem to you. In fact, what you are doing – mixing and matching different kinds of work – has a name. It is called portfolio working. Second, given that you will go on the books of an agency, our advice is to be absolutely straight with them. Tell them what you are looking to do and that you think this means you will want temporary work for however long (give a rough period of time). At the same time, tell them the days of the week on which you can work. Put all this information in your CV. Repeat it in any conversations you have with the agency and on any forms they ask you to fill in. Proceed on the basis of 'no misunderstandings' and hopefully you will go on to have a fruitful relationship with the agency.

Summary

Except in certain trades or professions, working for yourself was once considered to be an offbeat thing to want to do. Not so today where the patterns of an increasing number of careers frequently involve some time spent in self-employment. Sometimes these spells are short; sometimes they go on for long periods; and sometimes they lead to bigger things (most businesses started off with someone's dream to 'go it alone').

In this chapter we have urged you not to view yourself as divorced from the world of CVs just because you happen to work independently. Your CV still has a part to play in the advancement of your future, and we have drawn your attention to two situations where a good, well-put-together CV will help you to pave the way forward by:

• getting you business
• getting the support of financial institutions like banks.

We move in an increasingly professional world where people are very rarely taken on face value because of the risks involved. Today, it is far more likely that you will have to produce evidence of your competence before you're allowed to put your skills into practice, and your CV can play a vital part in this process.

10

moving forward with your CV

Use your CV to set the agenda

A CV isn't simply there to get you interviews. It goes on working for you, and in this chapter we will be showing you how.

Interviews

When you go for an interview, it is customary to find the interviewer seated behind a desk with your CV in front of him or her. If you have been asked to complete an application form at some point in the selection process leading up to the interview, then it is also customary to find that this is on the interviewer's desk.

Unless the interviewer has previous knowledge of you – for instance, if you've worked for the same organization before – your CV and/or application form will be the starting point for the dialogue that is about to open up. The interviewer will be assessing your suitability for the position in question, and the information in your CV and/or application form will determine:

- the direction of the interview
- the topics that come up for discussion
- the questions that are asked.

Interview questions

Interviewers vary enormously in their style and competence, but candidates often don't allow for the fact that many interviewers find the experience of sitting down in front of a complete stranger every bit as daunting as they do. Many line managers have had no formal training in interviewing other than going on the odd short course. What's more, they only get the chance to practise their interview skills occasionally (when there is a vacancy for staff in the area they control). The result in many cases is an interviewer who is not too sure about what line of questioning to follow, and so the natural inclination is to be led by what's in front of them – namely your CV and/or application form.

Notepad

Interviewers normally cast their eyes over candidates' CVs and/or application forms before the interview starts. Therefore, the information they've just read, is freshest in their minds and this will form the natural lead-in point to an interview.

Keep the focus on your key achievements and skills

Your CV will of course start with your name, address and personal information, and the next item to catch the interviewer's eye will be your key skills and achievements. You are on strong ground here because, if you've done a good job so far with the design of your CV, your key achievements and skills will reflect the matches between:

- the requirements for the job
- what you have to offer.

Immediately, the interview is off to a good start and the more time you spend talking about what makes you precisely the right candidate for the job, clearly the better it is going to be for you.

The halo effect again

We touched on the halo effect earlier in the book. Just to remind you, the halo effect describes the tendency to ignore flaws in candidates who make a good opening impression, and this applies equally to interviews. The interviewer effectively makes up his or her mind in the first few minutes, and anything later on in the interview which doesn't fit with the already formed favourable opinion will *either* be overlooked *or* relegated in importance.

Notepad

Remember halo effects can work in reverse. Classically, an interview that gets off on the wrong foot is a position from which it is difficult to recover. The interviewer has already formed an opinion of you and it will be hard to dislodge the thoughts from his or her mind.

Let your CV do the work for you

Candidates sensing the need to register their strong points at the start of an interview, often say to the interviewer, as soon as they get seated 'Shall I tell you a little bit about myself?' Out of politeness and/or uncertainty, the interviewer usually replies 'Yes' to this question, signalling the candidate to launch into a 20-minute presentation of their credentials. What's wrong with this approach? Simply that with any job application you are, to a large extent, guessing where the focus of any employer's interest lies, and by taking over an interview you run the risk of setting an agenda that has little relevance (watch out for the interviewer's glazed over expression!).

So what's the answer? Don't take over interviews. Instead, let your CV do the work for you. Allow the interviewer to decide the direction in which the interview is going to proceed, and in that way you can be sure that the direction is one relevant to the selection criteria for the job. Let interviewers focus on the aspects of your CV that interest them. Leave it to them to select which of your key skills and achievements they want to talk about. See your CV as a menu from which the interviewer can pick and choose items. Every item on selection is of course favourable to you.

Consistency and credibility

Your CV paints a glowing picture of you and your suitability for the job, but it won't do you much good if no one believes it. Credibility is an important issue at interviews, and one to which you must pay attention if you want your job applications to succeed.

How candidates let themselves down

Candidates go for interviews, psych themselves up beforehand, answer all the tough questions in the correct way, and feel at the end of it that they've put on a good performance. Then two weeks later, they receive a letter in the post telling them they have not been picked for a second interview. 'What went wrong?' they ask themselves. 'Did I put my foot in it and, if so, where?'

There are many reasons why perfectly good candidates fall by the wayside as the stages in a selection process unfold. A common one, however, is where the candidate loses the trust and confidence of the employer. The employer feels that they are not being told the truth, or only part of the truth, and understandably they don't feel inclined to take the discussions with the candidate any further.

The importance of consistency

How do these gaps in credibility arise? Often because of the simplest of reasons. Take the example of Simon A. Simon A is applying for the job of general manager in a construction company – a position for which he is well qualified. Simon A has not been in his present job for very long, and in his CV he has given 'broken promises' as his reason for wanting to leave. However, when the question, 'Why are you looking for another job?' is put to him at an interview, he answers by referring to disputes he is having with his chairman over the direction the business should be going in. A minor inconsistency? Perhaps, and perhaps Simon A has two problems with his present job – broken promises *and* a chairman who is standing in the way of progress. Should the person conducting the interview clear up the inconsistency by asking Simon A to explain? In an ideal world, possibly, but the fact is that many of these minor inconsistencies are allowed to pass and, though it may seem trivial, to an employer who has no previous knowledge of you such inconsistencies serve to sow seeds of doubt. What other questionable information is there in your CV? For instance, do you have all the qualifications you claim to have? Is your experience with a particular brand of software all that you are making it out to be? In what other ways have you embellished the truth to make your CV look more presentable?

Bearing in mind that in most cases you won't be the only candidate in line for the position and there will be plenty of others to choose from, the natural inclination for employers is to dispose of any candidates they feel they can't trust. They simply send out the standard 'sorry and no thank you' letter, and you are left to guess at the reason why your application got no further.

Key point
Keep the information consistent

Make sure that any information you give to an employer marries up with information you have given elsewhere, otherwise:

- your credibility suffers
- your chances of success are undermined.

In particular, pay attention to matching up information in:

- your CV
- your letter of application
- online applications
- any application forms you are asked to fill in
- any forms you fill in for consultants, e.g. registration forms for employment agencies
- statements you make at interviews.

Revisit your CV

It is important to revisit your CV before you write any letters of application or fill in any forms to make sure that the information you're providiing is the same throughout. Revisit your CV and other documents once more before you attend any interviews to refresh your memory about what you've said. Remember that in most cases interviewers will have your CV and/or application form in front of them while they're talking to you. They will see at a glance whether the answer you've just given to their question is consistent with the information you've written elsewhere.

Keep copies

Clearly you won't be able to carry out a pre-interview consistency check along the lines we suggest unless you have kept copies of all the relevant documents. In the case of your CV, this means keeping copies of the versions you use for each application you make. A tip is to have a dossier on each application, i.e. a file in which you put documents such as the ad for the job or any notes you took in your discussions with consultants together, of course, with the version of your CV that you used.

Warning

As we all know to our cost, PCs have the unfortunate habit of misbehaving themselves at the wrong moment, for example, the moment you have put aside to revisit your CV half an hour before you set off for your interview. Do not to rely on accessing information stored on a PC, floppy disk or CD, etc. at the last minute. Always print off two copies of your CV – one to send off with your application and one to keep in your dossier where you can access it easily, quickly and without any bother. Don't let the fact that your PC crashes be the reason you go into your interview poorly prepared.

Notepad

It is important to keep tabs on which version of your CV has been sent to which employer. This seems like a simple enough exercise, but problems can and do arise, notably where:

• you're put forward for a job by a consultant or an employment agency; where the version of your CV that has been sent to the employer is the one that was given to the consultant or agency when you registered with them and may not be: (a) up to date; or (b) consistent with your best efforts

- an employer has kept your CV on file either from one of your mailshots or from a previous application – again the information on it may not be up to date or consistent with how you now want to present yourself (in this context note that employers sometimes keep the CVs of interesting looking candidates for surprisingly long periods of time – often years)

- in pursuit of perfection you are constantly rehashing your CV so there are many variations in existence (a problem we will be looking at in greater detail in Chapter 11).

You are seeking to avoid at all costs sitting in front of an interviewer trying to fathom out which version of your CV he or she has got. Is it your latest or is it one you put together some time ago – one which is out of date or no longer conveys your aspirations? The difficulty is first that precious interview time is lost; and second and more importantly that the interviewer could be left with the impression that you are trying pull the wool over his or her eyes.

If you feel that an employer may be in possession of an obsolete CV, always offer to send in a new one *before* the interview. Don't do anything to queer the pitch at the start of an interview because those all-important early impressions will suffer.

Employers play safe

In today's world, employers are wary about who they offer jobs to. Why? There are two main reasons:

1 The increasing importance of team work in most businesses – a square peg can have an extremely disruptive effect.

2 We live in a litigation culture, and there is an increasing likelihood that sacking someone will result in having to defend a case in court or before an employment tribunal.

As a result, employers play safe when it comes to appointing new staff to the point where they don't take risks. This means avoiding anyone who fails to come across in a straightforward manner. People whose stories are inconsistent fall into this category – it is critical that all the information you give to employers forms one cohesive picture.

Questions and answers

Professional interviewers

Q *Not all interviewers are as you describe. Some are highly qualified and experienced and they won't be stumped when it comes to knowing what questions to ask. Am I right in thinking that your comments are confined to interviews conducted by 'amateurs' such as line managers?*

A To an extent, yes, but the anecdotal evidence we hear suggests that there are more interviews today that fit into the 'amateur' category than there were 20–30 years ago. As to 'professional' interviewers, they can be divided into two categories:

- Human resources specialists, i.e. managers employed by companies in what used to be known as the personnel function. Such managers will be trained and experienced in carrying out interviews, and are more likely to be found in larger firms (where the number of people employed justifies the need).

- Consultants, i.e. people who make a living out of recruitment and selection and who will be experienced for these reasons.

An important point to note about professionals is that they will tend to be 'generalists', whereas amateurs will tend to be line managers who may not have too much insight into interviewing but who will have an in-depth knowledge of the job for which you are applying. Are professionals more inclined to follow their own line of questioning rather than be led by the contents of your CV? Yes, but even in these situations don't discount the power of your CV to influence the agenda for the interview. Your CV will still be there sitting on the desk, and you can bet your bottom dollar that the professional will have spent some time before the interview poring over it.

Taking over interviews

Q *I take the point about taking over interviews but what about interviewers who start the interview by asking you to say a little about yourself? Isn't this inviting you to take over and, if so, how do you avoid going off on a track they won't find relevant or interesting?*

A One measure of a good interview is who does most of the talking. If it's the interviewer, then little has been accomplished, whereas if it's the interviewee then there will be a better chance of having sufficient information on which to base subsequent judgements. Getting you to say a bit about yourself at the start of an interview is a way of: (a) getting this process going; and (b) taking pressure off the interviewer and giving him or her time to sit back and listen to you give an account of yourself. How to handle the situation? Keep your account brief. Confine it to a few words about who you are, your key achievements (your bullet points) and why you're interested in the job. Unless you're invited to do so, don't go into a long chronology about the various jobs you've done because this is where you could find the interviewer's attention waning. If the interviewer is interested in what you did ten years ago when you were at Company Q then he or she will ask you.

Controlling the agenda may not be in your best interests

Q *Returning to what you said at the beginning of the book about it not being in your best interests to proceed with some applications, for example, where a job is outside your range of skills or experience and where at the outset this wasn't very clear. How do you reconcile being employer-friendly with controlling interview agendas which, as I understand it, means focusing the interviewer's attention via your CV on topics that will be favourable to you? Doesn't this mean you could end up getting a job that's unsuitable and, if so, what's the gain?*

A There is no gain, you are absolutely right. Indeed, a bad move is usually the prelude to all sorts of other misfortunes – not least the misfortune of you finding yourself out on your ear and facing the task of somehow getting your career back on track. However, there is a distinction between putting yourself across at an interview in your best possible light and seeking to pull the wool over employers' eyes by omitting facts or not making your career aspirations transparent. Many perfectly good candidates do not get beyond the first interview stage simply because they don't get their best points over, and this is a pity. Whilst this may be largely the interviewer's fault for not asking the right questions, it is at the same time incumbent upon candidates to make sure that their best points are mentioned prominently so that they will be picked up, i.e. on the front page of their CVs.

Summary

A CV is not only there to get you interviews as a lot of experts may suggest. It goes on working for you and in this chapter we have sought to demonstrate how a well-designed CV can:

- set the agenda for interviews
- ensure that your best points come across
- put you on course for getting the job.

We have looked at the importance of credibility and how the messages you put across at interviews have got to be consistent with the messages in any documentation you submit to employers, including the messages in your CV. We have seen how small areas of doubt can arise from seemingly harmless yet inconsistent statements, and how these areas of doubt can mushroom into serious misgivings about candidates – sufficient to rule them out of the running as far as further consideration is concerned.

Employers make judgements based on what's in front of them and, if that is: (a) good; and (b) consistent then, providing you fit the bill in other respects, you are well on your way to getting the job. Consequently, controlling the agenda is important, and your CV plays a crucial part in this.

CV management

In this chapter you will learn:
- the importance of keeping your CV updated
- how to measure your CV's performance
- about the perfect CV

Why CV management is important

CV management is about keeping your CV up to date so that it is ready for you to use when the need arises.

The stop–start approach

With the exception of those who are currently active on the job market, it's quite usual to find that people's CVs, even in framework form, are ones compiled some time ago. What happens is that they spend X number of years in a job, during which time the need for a CV never arises. As a consequence, the CV they last used is stored away in a drawer somewhere and doesn't see the light of day until circumstances change. The expected pay rise doesn't materialize. They are passed over for the promotion they felt was rightfully theirs. They get a new boss who they can't see eye to eye with or, worse still, they find that their name is on a redundancy list.

What next? Such people will feel that they need to put some irons in the fire. They feel they should put out feelers, send off some job applications, register with a few firms of recruitment consultants – all activities that call for a current CV. Then they find that their CV hasn't been updated for years:

- personal information has changed, e.g., they have a new telephone number and/or e-mail address
- further qualifications are incomplete, e.g. they've been on new courses or their membership of the professional body to which they belong has been upgraded
- career horizons have been redefined – what they were looking for in life all those years ago is totally different from what they are looking for now
- salary and salary aspirations have changed (almost by definition)
- recent job history is missing.

Key point
Be poised

If you are in this situation, before you can go out on the job market, you first face the task of putting the framework version of your CV back in order. Simple? Not when you're under pressure because you've see the job of your dreams advertised in the local paper and you want to send off an application straightaway, Not

---

when a consultant is pushing you to e-mail your CV immediately. Not when your job is under threat and you want to spread the word around your circle of contacts urgently. The temptation is to then succumb to the pressure and dash off a CV quickly. Inevitably, the result won't be consistent with your best efforts and this is why, in today's uncertain world, you must always be poised to launch yourself onto the job market at any time (who knows what's round the next corner?). Having a current CV available in framework form is an important part of 'being poised'.

Update your CV straightaway

The need for a CV can and will arise at times when you least expect it, and so it is always advisable to keep the framework version constantly updated. For instance, if you do gain a further qualification, one of your first actions should be to call your CV up on screen and make the necessary amendments. This means that when the need for a CV suddenly arises, you will only have the relatively simple task of fine-tuning your CV to the purpose for which you intend to use it. You won't be scratching your head trying to remember when you passed an exam or went on a course, or doing anything else to distract you from giving your CV its final polish.

Warning

With first impressions at stake, never submit to the temptation to update your CV by inserting handwritten information. The result is invariably a mess. This practice also points out people who have:

- one standard version of their CV
- run off dozens of copies of their CV.

The fact that the copies are there, sitting on a shelf, is an invitation to use them. The fact that they are out of date is seen to be something that can be got around with a bottle of correcting fluid and a ball-point pen. The simple message here is 'Don't'.

Measuring effectiveness

Finding that their job applications don't go anywhere is the signal to most people to take another look at their CV and see whether it could be improved in any way.

Failing to get interviews

The classic test of a CV's effectiveness is whether it succeeds in getting you interviews or not. According to the experts, if you don't get interviews, the chances are that your CV is to blame. Is this correct?

There are many reasons why candidates don't get interviews so, before jumping to the conclusion that your CV is at fault, go through the following checklist and see if there could be another explanation for your lack of success:

- Are you applying for jobs that are beneath you? Candidates who are seen by the employers as 'too good for the job' don't get interviews. Predictably, this is rarely explained. Candidates get the standard 'sorry but no thank you' letter and they're left scratching their heads for the reasons why. It seldom occurs to them that they are under-reaching.

- Are your applications long shots? Are you looking for a very high salary? Are you trying to get promotion into a job with responsibilities you have never held before? Are you trying to change careers? This is not a hint for you to stop what you're doing, but rather a reminder that the move you're seeking to make is intrinsically a difficult one where not getting interviews should be seen as practically the norm. The watchwords here are 'keep going'.

- Are you in a disadvantaged group? For example, are you over 50? Do you have a disability? Are there gaps in your range of skills and experience? Is there anything else in your background which could be off-putting to an employer? If you fall into any of these categories then, irrespective of the effort that goes into the design of your CV, getting interviews will always be difficult. Take heart in the fact that the right opportunity is waiting for you. Connecting with it may take a little longer, that's all.

- Can you be contacted? As we saw in Chapter 3, being there to take the calls is important in today's world of jobs. How would someone trying to make contact with you by phone get on? Would they find it difficult? If so, this could be the reason why you're not getting interviews, i.e. nothing to do with your CV.

- When replying to jobs that are advertised, are you following the rules? Are you sending your applications off quickly? Are you following the instructions in the advertisement?

- Are you putting too much emphasis on the advertised or visible job market where competition is at is greatest and where the chances of getting interviews are slimmest? The answer here is to focus more of your attention on the unadvertised sector, e.g. by sending out mailshots or by tapping into your networks.

> **Warning**
> Don't automatically assume that your CV is at fault when you find you're not getting interviews. Take other possible reasons into account before embarking on a major overhaul. Bear in mind that you could be scrapping a perfectly acceptable CV and replacing it with something inferior. In the business of CV management, change isn't aways for the better.

How to assess performance

With job hunting we recommend a holistic approach to assessing performance. This means not simply looking at one factor in isolation (e.g. your CV) but taking everything into account – your targeting, how you go about sourcing jobs, the nature of the niche area of the market that you are attacking – in short, start from scratch and re-examine the whole strategy. However, only do this at specified time intervals or, for instance, when you've submitted 20 job applications without getting an interview. Why? For the simple reason that there are so many 'X' factors in selection that you need to give any strategy a proper chance to work before deciding to abandon it.

> **Notepad**
> Chopping and changing by constantly reacting to negative events such as turn-down letters is never a good way to proceed with job hunting. Your strategy will lack any kind of continuity, making the task of assessing its performance impossible.

Twiddling and tweaking

Some people are changing their CVs all the time, not because anything substantial has happened to them or they've had no joy with their job applications, but because they decide that A might look better swapped round with B, or C ought to be given more prominence than D, and so on. Whilst this constant twiddling and tweaking seems harmless enough it can in fact lead to two difficulties:

1 Yet more versions of your CV in circulation adding to the chances of confusion (the problem we referred to in Chapter 10, with the question of 'Which version of my CV have you got?' becoming an issue at an interview).

2 The difficulty of never being able to accumulate enough evidence to see whether a particular version of your CV works for you or not.

> **Key point**
> Avoid constantly trying to gild the lily. If you want to appraise your CV, do it against what counts – its performance. Measured over a period of time, does your CV get you interviews for jobs that interest you? If it doesn't, it might need some attention. If it does, leave it alone.

The perfect CV

With CVs, one of the great twenty-first century myths is that there is an ideal model that beats all-comers, and most of this twiddling and tweaking is all about striving for perfection.

There is no such thing as the perfect CV, so put this idea out of your mind. CVs are about people, and what's good about people is their diversity. Yes, your CV has to perform a task for you but, providing it meets the ground rules set out at the start of this book (see p. 30) there is a lot of scope left to put yourself across in your own unique way. Remember what we said in Chapter 1 about standard off-the-shelf CVs and how they can be boring to read? Don't forget the engagement factors and how that 'little bit of you' in your CV serves to draw the interest of employers. The message? Without being off the wall, don't be afraid to be innovative with the design of your CV. Don't feel you have to put yourself across in a way that is not you just on the say-so of some expert. In this context, don't become one of those people who projects an entirely different image at an interview to the one that they project in their CV. The effect on interviewers will be to question what they're seeing, and the credibility upon which all successful job applications depends could be destroyed.

Where updating introduces a disadvantage

Q *Last month I picked up another endorsement on my driving licence, and I now have two and, since I work in sales, I realize that this information on my CV isn't going to help me when it comes to getting interviews. I take the point about being employer-friendly and not withholding information that could be relevant but I won't get jobs if I don't get interviews so, in this case, wouldn't it be best to leave the second endorsement off? If questioned later, could I simply say I forgot to update my CV? What do you think?*

A We're not too sure what you're suggesting: (a) to leave your CV as it stands with one endorsement on it; or (b) to strike out any reference to your driving licence and convictions? Of the two, (b) is preferable because it doesn't involve you in telling an untruth. What you need to bear in mind, however, is that (b) could get you into situations where your convictions come to light in the final stages of a selection process and, if the employer isn't impressed by your two endorsements, the time you spent on attending interviews, going through selections tests, etc. is wasted. Alternatively, an employer suitably impressed by your other fine attributes may be prepared to live with the possibility of you losing your licence, and this is presumably what you are banking on. Another strategy would be to postpone your job hunting activities until such time as the first endorsement expires. On the other hand, if you're desperate to make a move or your job is at risk, you may need to shift your sights to jobs where a driving licence isn't required – for example, jobs in internal sales. At the same time, you would have to take into account any need to lower your salary expectations. If you have to go down this road, console yourself with the thought that you can get your expectations back up again once the disadvantage posed by your two endorsements is removed.

Asking employers to give an opinion

Q *Why not simply ring employers up and ask why you didn't get picked for the interview? In this way you'll find out pretty quickly whether your CV is to blame for letting you down.*

A In a world where the reason for someone not getting a job can go on to become the subject of litigation, don't expect employers to be open and frank with you about why they decided to turn you down. It is far more likely that they will hide behind smokescreens like, 'There were other candidates who were more suitable', or will simply avoid taking your call. In short, it doesn't move you forward very far and in some instances the answer you get could set you off on a completely false trail. Moreover, bear in mind that it is not an employer's job to tell you whether your CV is any good or not, and don't be too surprised if some of them give you a sharp reminder that they're not paid to be careers advisers.

What constitutes success?

Q *In my case I've applied for around 20 jobs, got five interviews and so far received no offers of employment. Is this a signal for overhauling my job hunting strategy, including a fresh look at my CV?*

A It depends entirely on the difficulty of the market you are targeting. For example, if you're targeting a narrow sector of highly paid jobs, then it's reasonable to expect that you will be up against formidable competition. In such circumstances, five interviews from 20 applications is probably not bad going, and it would be a mistake to change your approach. Certainly your CV seems to be doing its job. Whether your interview skills are in need of a brush up is another question. Again, any evaluation of success depends on the size and calibre of the field you are entering.

Summary

In this chapter we have looked at CV management and in what circumstances making changes to your CV is and isn't desirable. On the one hand, we have seen that it is important to keep the framework version of your CV up to date so that it is ready for you to use if the need should arise. On the other hand, we have looked at the dangers of endlessly revising CVs which can become obsessive and distract candidates from forming a proper and more rounded view of where their efforts would be best placed.

Example A: a framework CV

Curriculum vitae	**Jane B 1**
Name	Jane B
Address	Flat 4 Quayside House River Street PORTCHESTER PC2 1AA
E-mail	janeb@xxx.com
Telephone	home xxxxx xxxxxx (after 6 p.m. – except Thursday) office xxxxx xxxxxx mobile xxxxx xxxxxx
Date of birth	10.12.1970

Key skills/achievements

Education

1981–1987	City Comprehensive School
1987–1990	Queens' Commercial College (part-time day release)
2000–present	Portchester College of Further Education (evenings)

Qualifications

GCE 'O' level: English Language (B), Business Studies (B), Geography (C), Art (D) (1987)

RSA Typewriting: Stages 1, 2 and 3 (1987–1990)
RSA English Language: Stages 1, 2 and 3 (1987–1990)
Pitman Shorthand: 90 and 100 w.p.m. (1988–1990)
RSA Word Processing: Stages 1, 2 and 3 (1999–2000)
RSA Teachers' Diploma in Administration Skills (2002)
D32/33 Assessors' Awards (2002)
RSA/OCR Integrated Business Technology Stage 3 (due to complete 2005)

IT skills

I am fully conversant with Microsoft Word, Excel, Access, PowerPoint and Publisher.

I act as the IT trouble-shooter in my present company. I am responsible for purchasing all hardware and software.

Ambitions

Salary

I currently earn £20K per annum. I am seeking a salary of £22K minimum.

Employment history

1995–present Portchester Building Supplies Limited

Position held: Secretary/PA to Managing Director. In addition to secretarial duties I am responsible for payroll and IT in a company with an annual turnover of £1.5m.

1988–1994 Martin & Associates

Position held: Administration Assistant in a small firm of solicitors. Telephone calls, correspondence, word processing letters, legal documents, etc. using Microsoft Word (initially self-taught),. Reason for leaving: to pursue ambition to become a Secretary/PA.

1987–1988 Furnival and Sons Limited

Twelve months' placement with a firm of paper merchants. General office duties: typing, filing, inputting data, etc. Reason for leaving: end of placement.

Period of notice

One month.

Nationality

British.

Marital status

Single.

Health

Good (non-smoker).

Leisure time activities

Swimming. Going to the theatre. Keeping fit – I visit the gym twice a week.

References

Work: Graham Martin, Senior Partner, Martin & Associates (tel: xxxxx xxxxxx)

Personal: June Griffiths, Senior Lecturer in Computer Studies, Portchester College of Further Education (tel: xxxxx xxxxxx)

Example B: a CV for attacking the competition

Curriculum vitae   **Jane B 1**

Name   Jane B

Address   Flat 4
Quayside House
River Street
PORTCHESTER
PC2 1AA

E-mail   janeb@xxx.com

Telephone   home xxxxx xxxxxx (after 6 p.m. –
except Thursday)
office xxxxx xxxxxx
mobile xxxxx xxxxxx

Date of birth   10.12.1970

Key skills/achievements

- I have worked in a senior position as a secretary/PA for the last ten years.
- I am conversant with all versions of Microsoft Word. I currently use Word 2000.
- My shorthand skills are proficient up to 100 w.p.m.
- I am fully flexible. My working day knows no boundaries. I have no ties and I am used to working long and unsociable hours.
- I hold a full clean driving licence.
- I am used to having access to highly confidential information. I am currently responsible for salaries and service contracts of senior staff. I attend board meetings and take minutes.
- I strive to keep my skills up to date by attending courses in my own time.

Education

1981–1987	City Comprehensive School
1987–1990	Queens' Commercial College (part-time day release)
2000–present	Portchester College of Further Education (evenings)

Qualifications

GCE 'O' level: English Language (B), Business Studies (B), Geography (C), Art (D) (1987)

RSA Typewriting: Stages 1, 2 and 3 (1987–1990)
RSA English Language: Stages 1, 2 and 3 (1987–1990)
Pitman Shorthand: 90 and 100 w.p.m. (1988–1990)
RSA Word Processing: Stages 1, 2 and 3 (1999–2000)
RSA Teachers' Diploma in Administration Skills (2002)
D32/33 Assessors' Awards (2002)
RSA/OCR Integrated Business Technology Stage 3 (due to complete 2005)

IT skills

I am fully conversant with Microsoft Word, Excel, Access, PowerPoint and Publisher.

I use the above almost on a daily basis. I am constantly striving to keep my skills up to date by attending evening classes.

Ambitions

I am seeking a position as a Secretary/PA in a larger organization where I will be working with a wider cross-section of people.

Salary

I currently earn £20K per annum. I am seeking a salary of £22K minimum.

Employment history

1995–present Portchester Building Supplies Limited

Position held: Secretary/PA to Managing Director. In addition to secretarial duties I have responsibility for payroll and IT.

1988–1994 Martin & Associates

Position held: Administration Assistant in firm of solicitors. Telephone calls, correspondence, word processing letters, legal documents, etc. using Microsoft Word (initially self-taught). Reason for leaving: to pursue ambition to become a Secretary/PA.

1987–1988 Furnival and Sons Limited

Twelve months' placement with firm of paper merchants. General office duties: typing, filing, inputting data, etc. Reason for leaving: end of placement.

Jane B 3

Period of notice

One month.

Nationality

British.

Marital status

Single.

Health

Good (non-smoker).

Leisure time activities

Swimming. Going to the theatre. Keeping fit – I visit the gym twice a week.

References

Work: Graham Martin, Senior Partner, Martin & Associates (tel: xxxxx xxxxxx)

Personal: June Griffiths, Senior Lecturer in Computer Studies, Portchester College of Further Education (tel: xxxxx xxxxxx)

Curriculum vitae   **Jane B 1**

Name   Jane B

Address   Flat 4
                      Quayside House
                      River Street
                      PORTCHESTER
                      PC2 1AA

E-mail   janeb@xxx.com

Telephone   home xxxxx xxxxxx (after 6 p.m. –
                      except Thursday)
                      office xxxxx xxxxxx
                      mobile xxxxx xxxxxx

Date of birth   10.12.1970

Key skills/achievements

- I have a good employment record with ten years' experience of working as a Secretary/PA at a senior level.
- I have a high level of IT proficiency and I am fully conversant with Microsoft Word, Excel, PowerPoint and other leading packages.
- I can do shorthand up to 100 w.p.m.
- I am fully flexible. I have no ties and I am used to working long and unsociable hours.
- I have D32/33 Assessors' qualifications.

Education

1981–1987   City Comprehensive School
1987–1990   Queens' Commercial College (part-
                   time day release)
2000–present   Portchester College of Further
                   Education (evenings)

Qualifications

GCE 'O' level: English Language (B), Business Studies (B), Geography (C), Art (D) (1987)

Jane B 2

RSA Typewriting: Stages 1, 2 and 3 (1987–1990)
RSA English Language: Stages 1, 2 and 3 (1987–1990)
Pitman Shorthand: 90 and 100 w.p.m. (1988–1990)
RSA Word Processing: Stages 1, 2 and 3 (1999–2000)
RSA Teachers' Diploma in Administration Skills (2002)
D32/33 Assessors' Awards (2002)
RSA/OCR Integrated Business Technology Stage 3 (due to complete 2005)

IT skills

I am fully conversant with Microsoft Word, Excel, Access, PowerPoint and Publisher.

Ambitions

I am seeking a position as a Secretary/PA in a larger organization where I will be working with a wider cross-section of people.

Salary

I currently earn £20K per annum. I am seeking a salary of £22K minimum.

Employment history

1995–present Portchester Building Supplies Limited

Position held: Secretary/PA to Managing Director. In addition to secretarial duties I have responsibility for payroll and IT in a company with an annual turnover of £1.5m.

1988–1994 Martin & Associates

Position held: Administration Assistant in a small firm of solicitors. Telephone calls, correspondence, word processing letters, legal documents, etc. using Microsoft Word (initially self-taught). Reason for leaving: to pursue ambition to become a Secretary/PA.

1987–1988 Furnival and Sons Limited

Twelve months' placement with firm of paper merchants. General office duties: typing, filing, inputting data, etc. Reason for leaving: end of placement.

Period of notice

One month.

Nationality

British.

Marital status

Single.

Health

Good (non-smoker).

Leisure time activities

Swimming. Going to the theatre. Keeping fit – I visit the gym twice a week.

References

Work: Graham Martin, Senior Partner, Martin & Associates (tel: xxxxx xxxxxx)

Personal: June Griffiths, Senior Lecturer in Computer Studies, Portchester College of Further Education (tel: xxxxx xxxxxx)

Example D: a CV for consultants

Curriculum vitae   **Jane B 1**

Name	Jane B
Address	Flat 4 Quayside House River Street PORTCHESTER PC2 1AA
E-mail	janeb@xxx.com
Telephone	home xxxxx xxxxxx (after 6 p.m. – except Thursday) office xxxxx xxxxxx mobile xxxxx xxxxxx
Date of birth	10.12.1970

Key skills/achievements

- I have ten years' experience of working as a Secretary/PA at a senior level.
- I am qualified to RSA Stage 3 in typewriting, word processing and English.
- I hold Pitman's qualifications in shorthand up to 100 w.p.m.
- I have a high level of IT proficiency and I am fully conversant with Microsoft Word, Excel, PowerPoint and other leading packages.
- I have D32/33 Assessors' qualifications.

Education

1981–1987	City Comprehensive School
1987–1990	Queens' Commercial College (part-time day release)
2000–present	Portchester College of Further Education (evenings)

Qualifications

GCE 'O' level: English Language (B), Business Studies (B), Geography (C), Art (D) (1987)

RSA Typewriting: Stages 1, 2 and 3 (1987–1990)
RSA English Language: Stages 1, 2 and 3 (1987–1990)
Pitman Shorthand: 90 and 100 w.p.m. (1988–1990)
RSA Word Processing: Stages 1, 2 and 3 (1999–2000)
RSA Teachers' Diploma in Administration Skills (2002)
D32/33 Assessors' Awards (2002)
RSA/OCR Integrated Business Technology Stage 3 (due to complete 2005)

IT skills

I am fully conversant with Microsoft Word, Excel, Access, PowerPoint and Publisher.

Ambitions

I am seeking a position as a Secretary/PA in a larger organization where I will be working with a wider cross-section of people.

Salary

I currently earn £20K per annum. I am seeking a salary of £22K minimum.

Employment history

1995–present Portchester Building Supplies Limited

Position held: Secretary/PA to Managing Director. In addition to secretarial duties I have responsibility for payroll and IT in a company with an annual turnover of £1.5m.

1988–1994 Martin & Associates

Position held: Administration Assistant in a small firm of solicitors. Telephone calls, correspondence, word processing letters, legal documents, etc. using Microsoft Word (initially self-taught). Reason for leaving: to pursue ambition to become a Secretary/PA.

1987–1988 Furnival and Sons Limited

Twelve months' placement with firm of paper merchants. General office duties: typing, filing, inputting data, etc. Reason for leaving: end of placement.

Period of notice

One month.

Jane B 3

Nationality

British.

Marital status

Single.

Health

Good (non-smoker).

Leisure time activities

Swimming. Going to the theatre. Keeping fit – I visit the gym twice a week.

References

Work: Graham Martin, Senior Partner, Martin & Associates (tel: xxxxx xxxxxx)

Personal: June Griffiths, Senior Lecturer in Computer Studies, Portchester College of Further Education (tel: xxxxx xxxxxx)

Example E: a CV for a headhunter

Curriculum vitae	**Jane B 1**

Name Jane B

Address Flat 4
Quayside House
River Street
PORTCHESTER
PC2 1AA

E-mail janeb@xxx.com

Telephone home xxxxx xxxxxx (after 6 p.m. –
except Thursday)
office xxxxx xxxxxx
mobile xxxxx xxxxxx

Date of birth 10.12.1970

Key skills/achievements

- I am a secretary/PA with ten years' experience of working at a senior level.
- I hold a Teachers' Diploma in Administration Skills.
- I hold D32/33 Assessors' qualifications.
- I have a complete up-to-date knowledge of business software including Microsoft Office (Word, Access, PowerPoint and Excel).
- I am currently studying for the RSA/OCR Stage 3 qualification in Integrated Business Technology.

Education

1981–1987	City Comprehensive School
1987–1990	Queens' Commercial College (part-time day release)
2000–present	Portchester College of Further Education (evenings)

Qualifications

GCE 'O' level: English Language (B), Business Studies (B), Geography (C), Art (D) (1987)

RSA Typewriting: Stages 1, 2 and 3 (1987–1990)
RSA English Language: Stages 1, 2 and 3 (1987–1990)
Pitman Shorthand: 90 and 100 w.p.m. (1988–1990)
RSA Word Processing: Stages 1, 2 and 3 (1999–2000)
RSA Teachers' Diploma in Administration Skills (2002)
D32/33 Assessors' Awards (2002)
RSA/OCR Integrated Business Technology Stage 3 (due to complete 2005)

IT skills

I am fully conversant with Microsoft Word, Excel, Access, PowerPoint and Publisher.

Ambitions

I enjoy my current role which is challenging and responsible, but I would welcome any move that enabled me to combine my secretarial, IT and trainer skills. I would also welcome the opportunity to work in a larger organization where there would be a wider spectrum of people and situations to deal with.

Salary

I currently earn £20K per annum. I would be looking for £25K with appropriate fringe benefits in any future position.

Employment history

1995–present Portchester Building Supplies Limited

Position held: Secretary/PA to Managing Director. In addition to secretarial duties I have responsibility for payroll and IT in a company with an annual turnover of £1.5m.

1988–1994 Martin & Associates

Position held: Administration Assistant in a small firm of solicitors. Telephone calls, correspondence, word processing letters, legal documents, etc. using Microsoft Word (initially self-taught). Reason for leaving: to pursue ambition to become a Secretary/PA.

1987–1988 Furnival and Sons Limited

Twelve months' placement with firm of paper merchants. General office duties: typing, filing, inputting data, etc. Reason for leaving: end of placement.

Period of notice

One month.

Nationality

British.

Marital status

Single.

Health

Good (non-smoker),

Leisure time activities

Swimming. Going to the theatre. Keeping fit – I visit the gym twice a week.

References

Work: Graham Martin, Senior Partner, Martin & Associates (tel: xxxxx xxxxxx)

Personal: June Griffiths, Senior Lecturer in Computer Studies, Portchester College of Further Education (tel: xxxxx xxxxxx)

Example F: a CV for changing careers

Curriculum vitae   **Jane B 1**

Name	Jane B
Address	Flat 4 Quayside House River Street PORTCHESTER PC2 1AA
E-mail	janeb@xxx.com
Telephone	home xxxxx xxxxxx (after 6 p.m. – except Thursday) office xxxxx xxxxxx mobile xxxxx xxxxxx
Date of birth	10.12.1970

Key skills/achievements

- I hold an RSA Teachers' Diploma in Administration Skills.
- I have D32/33 Assessors' Awards.
- I am currently studying for the RSA/OCR Stage 3 qualification in Integrated Business Technology.
- I am fully conversant with Microsoft Office. I have many years' experience of using these packages in commercial situations.

Education

1981–1987	City Comprehensive School
1987–1990	Queens' Commercial College (part-time day release)
2000–present	Portchester College of Further Education (evenings)

Qualifications

GCE 'O' level: English Language (B), Business Studies (B), Geography (C), Art (D) (1987)

RSA Typewriting: Stages 1, 2 and 3 (1987–1990)
RSA English Language: Stages 1, 2 and 3 (1987–1990)
Pitman Shorthand: 90 and 100 w.p.m. (1988–1990)

RSA Word Processing: Stages 1, 2 and 3 (1999–2000)
RSA Teachers' Diploma in Administration Skills (2002)
D32/33 Assessors' Awards (2002)
RSA/OCR Integrated Business Technology Stage 3 (due to complete 2005)

IT skills

I am fully conversant with Microsoft Word, Excel, Access, PowerPoint and Publisher.

Ambitions

I wish to pursue a career in teaching IT and administrative skills. I have attended courses in my own time and at my own expense to get the qualifications I need. I am now looking for the right opening.

Salary

I currently earn £20K per annum. I realize that I may not be able to command this level of salary in my first position.

Employment history

1995–present Portchester Building Supplies Limited

Position held: Secretary/PA to Managing Director. In addition to secretarial duties I have responsibility for payroll and IT in a company with an annual turnover of £1.5m.

1988–1994 Martin & Associates

Position held: Administration Assistant in a small firm of solicitors. Telephone calls, correspondence, word processing letters, legal documents, etc. using Microsoft Word (initially self-taught). Reason for leaving: to pursue ambition to become a Secretary/PA.

1987–1988 Furnival and Sons Limited

Twelve months' placement with firm of paper merchants. General office duties: typing, filing, inputting data, etc. Reason for leaving: end of placement.

Period of notice

One month.

Nationality

British.

Marital status

Single.

Health

Good (non-smoker).

Leisure time activities

Swimming. Going to the theatre. Keeping fit – I visit the gym twice a week.

References

Work: Graham Martin, Senior Partner, Martin & Associates (tel: xxxxx xxxxxx)

Personal: June Griffiths, Senior Lecturer in Computer Studies, Portchester College of Further Education (tel: xxxxx xxxxxx)

Example G: a CV for business

Curriculum vitae   **Jane B 1**

Name   Jane B

Address   Flat 4
                            Quayside House
                            River Street
                            PORTCHESTER
                            PC2 1AA

E-mail   janeb@xxx.com

Telephone   home xxxxx xxxxxx (after 6 p.m. –
                            except Thursday)
                            office xxxxx xxxxxx
                            mobile xxxxx xxxxxx

Date of birth   10.12.1970

Key skills/achievements

- I hold an RSA Teachers' Diploma in Administration Skills.
- I have D32/33 Assessors' Awards.
- I am able to train staff on most commercial packages including Mircrosoft Word, Excel, Access, PowerPoint and Publisher.
- I set up my own training business in August 2004 and I have already built up an impressive client list.
- I am fully flexible and able to meet a wide range of clients' needs. I am used to teaching mixed abilities from graduates to people with disabilities and learning difficulties.

Education

1981–1987   City Comprehensive School
1987–1990   Queens' Commercial College (part-
                            time day release)
2000–present   Portchester College of Further
                            Education (evenings)

Qualifications
GCE 'O' level: English Language (B), Business Studies (B), Geography (C), Art (D) (1987)

RSA Typewriting: Stages 1, 2 and 3 (1987–1990)
RSA English Language: Stages 1, 2 and 3 (1987–1990)
Pitman Shorthand: 90 and 100 w.p.m. (1988–1990)
RSA Word Processing: Stages 1, 2 and 3 (1999–2000)
RSA Teachers' Diploma in Administration Skills (2002)
D32/33 Assessors' Awards (2002)
RSA/OCR Integrated Business Technology Stage 3 (due to complete 2005)

Client list

I have carried out training and assessment assignments for the following leading clients:

- Highpoint Technologies Group
- Simmonds Construction Sealants plc
- Portchester Design Partnership
- Graphic Products Limited
- Avery & Sinclair plc.

Employment history

1995–2004 Portchester Building Supplies Limited

Position held: Secretary/PA to Managing Director plus IT co-ordinator. Reason for leaving: to set up in business as an IT trainer.

1988–1994 Martin & Associates

Position held: Administration Assistant in a small firm of solicitors. Reason for leaving: to pursue ambition to become a Secretary/PA.

1987–1988 Furnival and Sons Limited

Twelve months' placement with firm of paper merchants. Reason for leaving: end of placement.

Nationality

British.

Marital status

Single.

Health

Good (non-smoker).

Leisure time activities

Swimming. Going to the theatre. Keeping fit – I visit the gym twice a week.

References

John Wedderburn, Sales Director, Construction Sealants plc (tel xxxxx xxxxxx)

Stella Reeves, Administration Manager, Graphic Products Limited (tel xxxxx xxxxxx)

Points to note

Example A

1 From this framework version of her CV, we can see that Jane B has sought to widen her horizons by adding IT teaching qualifications to her portfolio of skills as a secretary/PA. We will see in the design of the examples that follow how she brings the range of her skills/qualifications into effect as she sets off in pursuit of different career aims.

2 Consistent with the advice in Chapter 3, Jane has left the key skills/achievements and personal ambitions sections of her framework CV blank.

3 Jane has given some thought to her contactability. She has given her e-mail address and telephone points of contact. She has advised recipients of her CV that she is not in on Thursdays (the evening she goes to college).

4 Her salary ambitions are clear.

Example B

1 In this version of her CV, Jane B is applying for the position of Secretary/PA to the Chief Executive of a large building society which has its head office in the city where she lives. The position was given prominent block advertising in the

local evening newspaper stating an 'excellent' salary together with a company car and a private health care plan (perks Jane doesn't currently enjoy). Jane realizes however that a job of this calibre is going to attract a large number of applicants and her CV needs to take account of this fact.

2 Jane has produced a good front page. The advertisement mentioned shorthand proficiency and experience with the word processing package that Jane refers to, together with the need to be flexible with hours. Jane has guessed that confidentiality is going to be an issue in a job role as a Secretary/PA to a Chief Executive and this is why she has included it as one of her bullet points. She has also guessed that the provision of a company car indicates that there will be a need for business travel hence the mention of her clean driving licence and the fact she has no ties.

3 Jane has made her salary ambitions clear.

4 Jane is probably in a rut with her present job but correctly she makes no mention of this. Instead, she talks about her wish to work in a larger organization with a wider cross-section of people, i.e. good positive points. Because of its size, the building society can offer the opportunity Jane is seeking and so the match between what she wants and what the employer can provide is made.

5 Jane's teaching qualifications clearly have no relevance to this particular application hence she has relegated them to a bare mention. The recent courses she has attended are put in the wider context of keeping her skills up to date.

6 The reference to the size of her previous employer has been taken out in case it should be seen as a negative point.

7 The fact that she is the IT trouble-shooter in her present company has also been taken out for the reason that it will have no relevance in a larger organization like the building society.

Example C

1 In this scenario, Jane B is sending out a mailshot to six large firms in her area to see if they have any suitable vacancies for secretaries/PAs. She is keen to ensure that any response she elicits is from employers who will be happy to pay her the £22K that she is seeking.

2 Jane's key skills and achievements have been given a different slant to take account of the fact that this version of her CV will be going to six different employers. She has therefore

brought into prominence all the software that she is familiar with, whereas in Example B it was only her experience with Microsoft Word that was relevant.

3 The qualifications she holds as an assessor and trainer are scarce skills and ones that could catch the eye of a prospective employer (a recipient of her mailshot). Although they had no relevance to the position in Example B, she is casting her net a little further this time and who knows?

4 If the recipient of her mailshot has (or might have) vacancies for secretaries/PAs then there is sufficient here to:

• see that she isn't a time-waster
• generate interest and make the reader want to turn over to the next page.

5 Her ambition is stated clearly. There should be no misunderstandings over what will or won't interest her.

6 Likewise, her salary ambitions are stated clearly. Again, there should be no misunderstandings.

Example D

1 Here Jane B has designed a CV for three employment agencies who specialize in appointments for secretaries and PAs. The hope is that they will find a suitable opening for her and Jane's task is to ensure that:

• their efforts are properly directed
• her most marketable talents are brought into prominence.

2 Key skills and achievements are spelt out graphically so that the right matches are made in any file searches

3 The skills and achievements listed are those that are likely to be of most interest to agency clients (her best-selling features).

4 Again, her ambitions are clearly stated. There should be no excuse for any mismatches.

Example E

1 Jane has received a phone call from a headhunter (someone she has never heard of before). The headhunter is asking if she is interested in a position with a leading client – a multinational with offices that are within commuting distance of where Jane lives. Although the headhunter won't divulge the name of the client he indicates that a salary of £25K plus company car would be available. He says that he has been given Jane's name by a mutual acquaintance because she has a blend of secretarial and trainer skills that

will interest his client. He is keen to take matters further but first he wants Jane to send in a CV.

2   Jane has completely changed the direction of her CV. She has brought her trainer skills into greater prominence than they have been given previously.

3   Although she doesn't know much about the position, she has taken into account the headhunter's remarks about what earmarked her for the approach.

4   Conversely she has given a little less prominence to her secretarial/PA skills.

5   In her ambitions section, she has established that there is a match between what she is seeking in career terms and what the headhunter's client seems to have to offer.

6   She has upped her salary expectations so she is starting off the negotiation at the right level (getting the best deal for herself).

Example F

1   Jane B has decided that she doesn't want to be a secretary/PA any more. She has decided instead that she wants to pursue a career as an IT teacher/trainer and she needs someone to give her a break. This version of her CV is designed for this purpose.

2   Jane's CV has been completely turned around. Her teaching qualifications have now been brought to the foreground, and her experience as a Secretary/PA has been pushed to the background.

3   Jane has made it clear in her ambitions section that she is seeking a change of career. At the same time, she has indicated the steps she has taken to realize her ambition. The fact that she has footed the bill for her training and done it in her own time is all part of the task of convincing employers that she is serious.

4   She has addressed the concerns that employers may have about her salary. She has stated in her CV that she is prepared to take a drop in earnings if this is necessary.

Example G

1   Jane has decided to go it alone as a self-employed IT trainer. She gave notice to Portchester Building Supplies and left them six months ago. She is already doing work for several companies including two of Portchester's suppliers (people

she approached when she was still in her old job). She is now looking for more business and has designed a CV to give to her prospective clients.

2 Her key skills and achievements are entirely focused on her role as a training service provider.

3 She has included a client list in her CV.

4 Her employment history has been updated and the detail stripped out (not relevant).

5 Sections dealing with ambitions, salary and period of notice have been taken out because they have no relevance.

6 Jane's referees are two of her clients (people who she knows will put in a good word for her). Recipients of this version of her CV will mainly want to now how she performs as a trainer, and the two people named will be able to provide this information, i.e. it is relevant.

7 She makes it clear that she left Portchester Building Supplies to start her own business. Recipients of her CV will be able to see from this that she is committed to making a success out of being a service provider, i.e. she is not doing it as a stopgap while she is looking for another job as a secretary/PA.

taking it further

Books

A glance at the website of any major bookseller will reveal just how many titles there are on writing CVs. Here is a short selection of some of the better known ones:

CVs in a week, Steve Morris and Graham Willcock, Hodder & Stoughton/Chartered Management Institute, 1998.

How to Write a Winning CV, Alan Jones, Random House Business Books, 2001.

30 Minutes to Prepare Your CV, Lynn William, Kogan Page, 2002.

Brilliant CVs: What Employers Want to See and How to Say It, Jim Bright and Joanne Earl, Prentice Hall, 2001.

The Perfect CV, Tom and Ellen Jackson, Piatkus Books, 1991.

Write a Winning CV, Julie-Ann Amos, How To Books, 2003.

The two books in the Teach Yourself series written by ourselves and referred to in the text are:

Managing Your Own Career, 2003.

Making Successful Career Changes, 2001.

Particularly when scanning the shelves in public libraries, beware any books on CVs that were written some time ago. The advice in them may not be relevant to modern conditions.

Learning from other people's ideas

You may be involved in recruiting staff as part of your work. In which case you will have the opportunity to see CVs that candidates have sent in, and you can learn from their efforts. You will see which CVs catch the eye and which don't. Other people's ideas can sometimes be better than your own. You can apply what you learn to the design of your own CV.

index